In The Asking, I Changed - 2

OrangeBooks Publication

1st Floor, Rajhans Arcade, Mall Road, Kohka, Bhilai, Chhattisgarh 490020
Website: **www.orangebooks.in**

First Edition, 2025

ISBN: 978-93-6554-048-2

Price: Rs. 349.00

Printed in India

In The Asking, I Changed 2

Charrvi Singh

OrangeBooks Publication
www.orangebooks.in

Preface

We are raised to believe that certainty is strength … that answers are destinations and questions mere detours. But what if the questions shape us more than anything else? What if wondering and sitting in the discomfort of not knowing is where we truly begin?

This journey began with a question I couldn't answer. Then came another. And another. Each one tugged at something, an old belief, a quiet grief, a half-formed truth I had been carrying without noticing. I started writing to untangle them, thinking I was searching for clarity. What I found instead was something messier and far more honest.

At first, I wanted to fix it, to name it, to make it make sense. Then I let it be. In that disarray, there was a strange kind of permission. I didn't have to know everything. I could let the questions breathe. Slowly, the writing shifted … from searching for something solid to sitting with what stirred.

Each thread that came loose revealed something I had forgotten I was made of. It didn't come gently. These pages clawed their way out of the chaos, not as a fix, but as a companion. Not a path to follow, but a feeling to return to.

This is not a book of conclusions. It is an exploration … emerging from the mess, and anchored in the honest, unfinished work of becoming. It wanders through the places we rarely sit with for long and asks: Who are they really for?

Each chapter begins not with a declaration, but with a wondering. And it ends with more. Because life rarely ties itself into a perfect bow. Sometimes, what we need isn't resolution, but resonance. A soft place to admit we're still becoming. A mirror that doesn't reflect certainty, but curiosity.

I don't know if you'll find answers in these pages. But I hope you find company. I hope you find questions that feel familiar. I hope you feel a little less alone in the not-knowing.

Because somewhere between what we're told to believe and what we begin to ask, there's a quiet revolution happening.

***I changed*, not when I found answers,**

But *in the Asking.*

Table of Contents

Why Can't I Start?

Is it the pull of a dream, or the push of fear? Is it passion in its purest form, or a quiet panic that we might waste our only chance?

The Cambridge Dictionary defines motivation as the enthusiasm for doing something. But if you dig deeper, the word traces back to movere, Latin for "to move." Motivation is movement. Not always forward. Sometimes it's side-stepping doubt. Sometimes it's dragging ourselves through mud.

In psychology, motivation is the internal force that propels us toward goals. Maslow's hierarchy tells us we climb through needs like rungs on a ladder … from survival to self-actualisation. Herzberg separates what pushes us from what pulls us: satisfaction on one side, avoidance of misery on the other.

But theories feel tidy. Life, of course, doesn't.

A lifelong musician once greeted the day with music instead of alarms. But something changed.

She woke before sunrise, the air still cold, the city not yet stirring. Her violin leaned quietly in the corner, strings slightly out of tune. Her fingers hovered over it, then lowered. She made coffee instead. She used to practice every morning, music flooding the flat before breakfast. Now the silence rang louder. She still loved it. But something had changed. It wasn't laziness. It was a kind of ache, hard to name. What happened to the girl who once played through fever, heartbreak, thunder?

Is it motivation that's missing? Or something deeper?

The poet Mary Oliver once asked: *Tell me, what is it you plan to do with your one wild and precious life?*

But some mornings, the more urgent question is: *how do I even get out of bed?*

Maybe we've misunderstood motivation. Maybe it isn't a constant flame, but a match we keep having to strike. Sometimes it sparks against joy. Other times, fear. Often, it fizzles out before we even notice.

Can motivation be trained like a muscle? Or is it more like weather … unpredictable, often inconvenient, occasionally glorious?

We like to assume those who succeed are more motivated. But what if they're simply better at navigating the droughts?

There was a surgeon scrubbing in for her twelfth hour, eyes red from strain. She was exhausted. She didn't feel motivated. But she moved anyway. Commitment held her up where motivation wouldn't.

And what about a single parent working two jobs, not because they woke up inspired, but because love demanded it. Is that motivation as well? Or need?

Then there was a student battling depression, who turned in just one assignment … not because they felt ready, but because showing up, even once, felt like resistance.

These aren't stories of peak motivation. They're stories of grace under fatigue. Which raises a deeper question: do we need motivation, or do we need meaning?

Viktor Frankl, psychiatrist and Holocaust survivor, wrote:

Those who have a 'why' to live can bear with almost any 'how.'

His work suggests that purpose outlasts motivation. That we move not because of enthusiasm, but because of significance.

So where does that leave the artist who hasn't painted in weeks? Or the once-ambitious teen who now scrolls aimlessly, wondering if they've peaked too early? Are they broken, or just overwhelmed? Maybe it's not a lack of drive, but a lack of clarity.

Sometimes, we don't know what to chase because we've been chasing too many things at once.

Or maybe we're afraid. Not of the work, but of what the work might reveal … that we're not as talented as we hoped. That we're running out of time. That success might isolate us more than failure ever did.

Can fear masquerade as laziness? Can confusion look like apathy?

We often treat motivation like a magic switch. On or off. But what if it's a *dimmer*, sensitive to everything ... sleep, grief, hormones, shame? What if motivation is less about willpower and more about gentle self-alignment?

Psychologist Edward Deci, in his Self-Determination Theory, separates motivation into intrinsic and extrinsic. Intrinsic motivation…when we act out of joy or deep interest…tends to last. Extrinsic, like praise or punishment, burns hot but briefly. So why do we still dangle carrots and wield sticks, expecting transformation?

The problem with external motivators is that they work…until they don't.

An employee performing for bonuses, yet burning out quietly when the applause stopped.

A child praised only for high marks, who learned to fear failure more than they loved learning.

What if we built motivation from care instead of pressure?

And still, some days, nothing works. No quote. No playlist. No to-do list crafted at 2 a.m. On those days, is it okay to rest? Is the rest a part of the movement, too?

Marcus Aurelius wrote in Meditations, *"You have power over your mind, not outside events. Realise this, and you will find strength."*

The Stoics believed motivation wasn't about feeling ready, but choosing to act anyway…not because success was guaranteed, but because virtue demands effort.

But modern life bombards us with performance metrics, comparison, and urgency. Our value is tied to output. No wonder we hesitate to begin when everything feels like a scoreboard.

Sometimes, starting feels less like taking the first step and more like standing at the edge of a pool in early spring … water glinting in sunlight, but the memory of winter still in the air. We want to dive in, but we keep imagining the shock of the cold. We wait for courage to arrive fully formed, forgetting that courage often only shows up after we move.

But what if we've been taught to begin only when we're ready? And what if "*ready*" never comes?

There's a strange comfort in not starting … the comfort of never being wrong, never disappointing ourselves. But it's also the slow ache of wondering what might have been. Which is worse? The sting of failure, or the dullness of regret?

Motivation doesn't just depend on what we want … it depends on how safe we feel wanting it. Neuroscience tells us the brain is wired to avoid threat more urgently than it seeks reward. If our goals feel like danger … social risk, emotional exposure, possible humiliation … the brain whispers *"stay still."*

And yet … movement happens in small ways too.

The artist who hadn't painted for months, but still rearranged her brushes each morning … as if keeping them close might keep the spark alive.

A runner who couldn't bear to train, but still bought new laces, just in case.

Sometimes, the rituals around the thing keep us tethered to it, even when the doing feels far away.

The danger is in mistaking waiting for preparation. Waiting can be an active choice, but more often, it's disguised fear.

What if, instead of asking *"Am I ready?"* we asked *"Am I willing?"*

Willing to risk the awkward first draft, the shaky performance, the unpolished beginning.

Once I saw a writer sitting in a café, a laptop open in front of him, the smell of roasted coffee curling into his sweater. The waitress told me he'd been telling people he was working on a novel for years. His fingers rested on the keys, unmoving. He ordered another drink. Checked the headlines. Reopened the same document, still stuck on the first page. For him, starting meant making it real. And making it real meant letting it be judged.

An employee was working in the same cafe who wanted to leave her job. Each Sunday night, her stomach knotted, but she still stayed. She scrolled job boards at midnight, saved listings, then deleted them. She told herself she was waiting for the right opportunity. In truth, she was afraid that even if she left, she'd carry the same emptiness somewhere else.

I met a teenager once in a metro who dreamed of applying to art school. He drew every day in secret but hid his sketches when anyone entered and tried to see. The thought of someone disliking his work felt heavier than never sharing it at all.

These stories aren't about laziness … they're about the fragile space between desire and action, the place where fear and longing sit side by side.

The surgeon I spoke about is a friend. She once laughed when I asked how she stayed motivated through such long, draining days. *"I'm not motivated,"* she said. *"I'm committed. There's a difference."*

Commitment shows up even when the spark is gone. Motivation is fickle. Commitment can be stubborn in the best way.

But how do we commit when we haven't started? How do we plant roots in something we're still circling from a distance?

Maybe by shrinking the distance. The first step doesn't have to be grand … it just has to happen. The violinist doesn't need to play the entire concert. She can pluck a single string, let the note hang in the air, and see what it stirs.

What if the beginning isn't the whole page, but the first sentence?

Not the marathon, but the first lap?

Not the novel, but a paragraph written in the corner of a receipt?

When we strip away the weight of the imagined ending, the start becomes lighter.

And sometimes, the reason we can't start is that we've lost sight of why we wanted to in the first place. Frankl's *"why"* isn't a fixed point … it changes with seasons, with age, with what we've survived.

The dream we had at 20 might not be the dream we need at 35. But letting go of an old dream can feel like betrayal. So, we keep circling it, not starting, but not releasing it either.

The violinist looked at her instrument again. She was older now, the fire of youth replaced by something softer, but steadier. Maybe she didn't want to play to impress anyone anymore. Maybe she just wanted to fill her apartment with sound on a quiet morning. Was that enough? Could it always have been enough?

We chase the perfect time, the perfect energy, the perfect self. But the truth is, we begin in imperfect kitchens, with coffee gone cold, under light that makes us squint. We begin with doubt in our chest and half-belief in our hands.

Maybe that's all a beginning really is … a moment where action outruns fear by just a fraction of a second.

She sets down her coffee. Lifts the violin. The first note is hesitant, almost shy, but it exists now. It cuts through the silence. The match has been struck.

It's not a roaring fire. But it's movement. And maybe, right now, that's enough.

In the quiet asking, we may begin to see that motivation isn't a lightning bolt.

It's a soft return.

A decision made in tired moments. A hand reaching for the brush, the book, the task … not because it feels good, but because something inside still whispers: *this matters*.

We're not meant to always move fast. We're just meant to keep moving … sometimes with purpose, sometimes with curiosity, sometimes with trembling hope.

In the asking, I changed.

And maybe that's what finally moved me.

Blank Page

Why does limitless potential paralyse us? Why does abundance, the very thing we thought would set us free, so often tighten its grip around us?

When the horizon opens wide with possibility, why does the body fold inward and the breath hold itself hostage?

You can feel it in the quiet before beginning. The air feels too still, as if waiting for instruction. Hands hover above the keyboard, palms faintly damp. The pencil rests above the page, its tip sharp enough to feel like pressure. The cursor blinks like a slow metronome, each flash louder than the last. The coffee beside you has gone cold, its bitterness filling the air with a faint reminder of time passing. The laptop light is sterile, blue-white and unkind. The hum of the ceiling fan turns rhythmic, like a small reminder that everything else is already in motion…except you.

The blank page doesn't just ask for ink. It asks for courage.

Maybe that's what makes it terrifying … that still moment before the first mark, when every path is possible and none yet chosen. Once you begin, you've narrowed the world. The perfect vision that lived untouched in your mind must now face translation, imperfection, and the limits of skill. Creation is an act of exposure. And exposure feels like risk.

Is it failure we fear … or success?

Failure invites shame, but success demands maintenance. You can trip once and move on, but to succeed is to become visible. To be seen is to be measured.

The blank page, in its stillness, whispers that the easiest way to avoid disappointment is never to begin.

An artist knows this intimately. She still rearranges her brushes every morning. She's been dreaming of a canvas for weeks … the way she'll let colour bleed into silence, the shade of blue she's imagined in her sleep.

When the linen finally stands before her, the room smells faintly of turpentine and morning light. She holds the brush, but her wrist won't move. The teacher's old warning echoes, "*Don't waste paint.*"

The critics, invisible but present, crowd the corners of her mind. Her palms sweat. She folds her hands and tells herself she'll start tomorrow. The truth is simpler. The longer she waits, the safer the vision feels.

One of my close friends, now an entrepreneur, told me how she once sat in a co-working space. A slideshow glows on the screen, its first slide blank, the title box blinking in quiet defiance. The hum of other laptops becomes a pulse of expectation.

She thinks of investors, of rent, of people waiting for her to have the right words. But all she can hear is the thud of her own heartbeat in her ears.

She wants to type *"Our Story,"* but her fingers hover, frozen between fear of overpromising and fear of not being believed.

I was in an exam hall, and I noticed my best friend unfold the exam sheet. The paper is cool and smooth beneath his fingertips. The scent of fresh ink clings to the pages. Around us, pens scratch and chairs creak, but his mind goes silent, evident as he stared into the blank sheet.

The page isn't freedom; it's exposure. His throat tightens.

Every question feels like a test not of knowledge, but of self.

What if he's not who he thought he was?

A musician sits at her desk. Her guitar leans against the wall, strings dull from neglect.

She adjusts the tuning pegs out of habit, listening to the faint, metallic hum. A single note hangs in the air and disappears too quickly. The silence afterwards feels heavier than sound.

She wants to begin, but her chest feels tight, her hands restless. The first note, she thinks, must be perfect. But perfection has no rhythm.

The blank page isn't just an object. It's a landscape of sound, scent, and memory … a place where ghosts of expectation live. It smells like pencil shavings and burnt toast, like every morning someone meant to start something and didn't. It's charged not only by what could be made, but by the weight of what's already imagined.

Perfectionism sits like a guardian at the gate, pretending to protect you while actually keeping you out. We call it *"standards."* We call it *"taste."*

But often it's fear in disguise, wearing the polite clothes of refinement.

It tells you not to embarrass yourself, not to waste materials, and not to show anything unfinished. Yet everything we love … from first drafts to first dates…begins unfinished.

Would we still chase perfection if we knew it was a form of procrastination dressed in discipline?

Psychologists call it the paradox of choice … the idea that too much freedom can freeze us. The blank page holds infinite options. Every possible line, word, or tone lies waiting. Our brains crave edges. Without them, we lose orientation. Maybe constraints aren't prisons. Maybe they're railings on a staircase too steep to climb without support.

A chef once told me he never starts with a full pantry. "*I cook best when I have only three ingredients*," he said, rolling up his sleeves. "*Too much freedom makes bad soup.*" He laughed softly, the smell of garlic already rising in the air. Maybe creativity doesn't expand in endless space, but in smaller kitchens … with just enough salt to taste the truth.

Blank pages exist everywhere. They aren't confined to paper.

A woman leaves a long marriage and finds herself sitting in a quiet apartment. The fridge hums too loudly. The bed feels foreign in its new silence. She is staring at a blank page.

A man retires after forty years of routine and wakes up to a day with no alarm clock, no calls, no instructions. The sunlight hits the curtains differently. Blank page.

Even grief holds its own blankness. The house is quieter. The toothbrush remains in its holder. The dinner table has one empty chair. There's an ache in the air that smells faintly of old perfume and absence. The blankness after loss is not creative … it's cavernous. And yet, it demands the same thing art does: to start again, however clumsily.

Who do we become when life stops giving us outlines to trace?

Perhaps that's why we cling to old patterns … because they are annotated. Predictable pain feels safer than unmarked peace.

The woman who had stayed in the cafe job she hated now found herself staring at another kind of blankness. The thought of updating her resume made her heart race. It wasn't laziness. It was terror…the terror of the empty document, the unfilled "Experience" box. The blankness of reinvention.

Every beginning implies an ending somewhere else. Every new identity requires the burial of an old one. No wonder our hands tremble before the first mark.

We romanticise starting over … the *"fresh start,"* the *"new chapter."*

But beginnings rarely glow. They stutter. They ache. Starting over is not cinematic. It's tender, awkward, alive.

Maybe the problem isn't blankness, but our need to fill it too quickly. The blank page might be asking for patience…for a breath before action, a pause before noise.

Could emptiness be sacred?

Sometimes the blankness isn't absence, it's incubation. The musician's pause before the chorus, the painter's step back to see the canvas from afar, the friend who takes a night to respond instead of rushing an answer … these moments aren't avoidance. They're care.

Can stillness be productive? Can waiting be a form of trust?

A poet I once knew wrote one line a day. Some days, it was nonsense. Some days, it was a single word. But after months, her notebook became a landscape of attempts. When she finally published a collection, she said, "*It wasn't a book of poems. It was a book of returns.*"

Maybe that's what every blank page really asks … not for brilliance, but for return.

Ritual helps.

A friend told me she lights a candle before writing. "*If nothing comes,*" she said, "*at least the room feels kind.*" I think of that often … the flame as a small contract between fear and grace.

The candle flickers near her desk. The air smells faintly of wax and paper. A teacup leaves a faint ring on the corner of her notebook. She breathes, once, twice. The page feels less like a threat and more like an invitation.

Ritual doesn't guarantee perfection. It guarantees arrival.

Perhaps the blank page isn't our enemy at all. Perhaps it's our most honest mirror … one that reflects not what we lack, but what we long for.

It asks quietly:

What are you afraid to say?

What would you risk if you said it badly?

What if you began, not to impress, but to understand?

Even the failures count. Edison's notebook was filled with dead ends. Writers' floors are littered with drafts. Painters paint over yesterday's doubts. These aren't failures. They're echoes of persistence…reminders that movement itself is meaningful.

A teacher once asked her students to draw the ugliest picture they could. The room filled with laughter, relief, and then … unexpectedly … beauty. The pressure dissolved the moment perfection was forbidden.

We confuse creation with performance. But performance comes later. Creation is rehearsal. It's the unfiltered conversation between who you are and who you might become. The blank page is that first meeting … awkward, unfinished, honest.

So, begin badly. Begin softly. Begin anyway.

Start with an honest line, not a clever one. Start with curiosity, not confidence. Let it wobble. Let it breathe. The blank page doesn't demand certainty; it only asks for your presence. And, remember: silence isn't the same as stillness. One is fear. The other is waiting.

If the page is blank, it's not accusing you … it's inviting you. You are not behind; you are on the brink.

So, take the smallest step you can. Write one line. Speak one truth. Make one mark. Even the tiniest gesture interrupts the tyranny of hesitation.

The blank page is a terrifying generosity. It holds nothing and promises everything. It is the quiet space between who you are and who you could be. It will not fill itself … but it will wait. Always.

In the asking, I changed.

And I learned that beginnings are not noise, but calm acts of returning to life.

Truth Turns Quiet

What is integrity, really?

Not in theory, not in textbooks, not in the neat compartments of a dictionary, but in the deeply human moments when everything you believe begins to unravel.

Is integrity just honesty dressed up in discipline?

Or is it something far less certain, something alive, something that stirs in the silence between what we feel and what we're expected to do?

We're told that integrity is about staying firm. But what if it is also about softening? About bending, not because our values are weak, but because we are paying close attention to the ache between principle and compassion.

What if integrity is not a fixed trait, but a conversation with ourselves that keeps evolving with every season of life? What if it is not something we have, but something we shape …

slowly, awkwardly … through each uncomfortable decision?

The dictionary calls it moral uprightness. Unshakable. Virtuous. The kind of thing a hero wears like armour. But life, as it turns out, doesn't often cast us as heroes. It gives us paradoxes. It offers no musical cue, no swelling strings to help us choose the high road. Just a split-second decision, and a silence that follows.

Integrity doesn't feel like armour in those moments. It feels like standing barefoot in the cold. You ask yourself what the right thing is, and somehow, in the very asking, you become someone else.

That's the part no one warns you about. That the asking itself begins to change you.

We like to believe our values are permanent. Anchored. Immune to the mess. But more often than not, they shift…quietly, unannounced … moved by context, fatigue, longing, fear. Do we call that hypocrisy? Or do we call it growth?

Convenience, too, plays its role quietly. We tell the truth when it suits us. We omit when the full truth might cast us in a harsher light. We speak up when it costs us nothing, and fall silent when the risk is too high. Is that dishonesty, or just being human? And if it's human, does that make it forgivable … or more dangerous?

My team lead, I saw her sitting in her parked car, keys still in the ignition, hands on the steering wheel, maybe not yet ready to walk into the building. Because A choice awaited her inside.

Lie to protect someone in trouble, or tell the truth and watch the fallout land elsewhere. Either way, someone would get hurt. She chose honesty. It felt noble, clean. But the consequences missed her and hit someone she cared for.

Later that night, while scrubbing a coffee cup that wasn't even dirty, she whispered into the sink, *"Was that integrity, or just me trying to save myself and calling it something noble?"*

So, was that integrity or just self-preservation in a better outfit?

We all like to believe we are honest. But honesty, when inconvenient, becomes something else. We bend it. We dress it up in good intentions. We justify. We revise memories. We cling to the parts that serve our image, and let go of the rest.

Is there such a thing as an honest omission? Or is that phrase just comfort hiding behind clarity?

This is where ideals tangle with reality. Sometimes, integrity demands truth. Other times, compassion urges us to blur the lines.

We are left in that gap, asking:

Who does this hurt?

Who does it protect?

Can I live with the version of myself that this decision creates?

And what about the lies we tell ourselves? The half-truths we tuck under the surface because naming them would rupture something too tender? We say we're doing the best we can. We say it didn't matter that much. We say we didn't know better. But deep down, some part of us always knows. Is integrity just the courage to face what you already know, even when it hurts?

Even philosophy stumbles here.

Kant says: Act only on principles you would want to become universal laws. Truth above all, no matter the cost. But life rarely rewards such purity. Sometimes it punishes it.

And so, Utilitarianism counters: let the outcome guide you. Choose the greatest good, even if it bends a few rules. But what if the *"greater good"* comes at the cost of someone's dignity? What if silence protects many but crushes one?

Neither framework feels complete when the stakes are personal. Perhaps they aren't meant to be answers, just starting points for better questions.

Perhaps integrity is not about choosing a side, but about daring to ask what each moment really needs.

And accepting that sometimes, that answer may crack something in you before it builds anything new.

What if integrity isn't a trait we have, but a mood we visit? A fleeting clarity that arrives in stillness, but slips away when urgency returns? How many truths have we set aside for later, hoping the moment will come back in simpler conditions?

We hold up certain people as moral giants … Gandhi, Lincoln, Mandela … as if they walked a straight line. But they didn't. They questioned. They hesitated. They made decisions that brought pain. Their greatness didn't come from certainty. It came from staying in the discomfort long enough to choose with care.

Gandhi's nonviolence was tested by cruelty. Lincoln wrestled with unity and emancipation. Mandela's clarity was forged through years in a cell, doubt echoing louder than certainty.

Their legacy may not lie in how unwavering they were, but in how deeply they grappled with what was right. Integrity, in that sense, isn't a straight path. It's a spiral. We return to the same questions again and again, but from a slightly different version of ourselves each time.

And sometimes, integrity isn't noble at all. Sometimes it's ugly. It looks like admitting you were wrong before anyone else sees it. Like turning in a friend. Like breaking a promise, you never should've made. It looks like telling the truth even when the truth makes you look cruel, or foolish, or hypocritical. Sometimes it means losing the thing you wanted most, because keeping it would require you to lie. Even now, in quieter times, the questions remain.

A whistleblower clicks "send" on a document that might ruin their career. They don't do it because, they are sure. They do it because they can't ignore the ache anymore. They ask themselves, "*Can I stay silent and still call myself whole*"?

That question alone begins to undo them.

Or take Oskar Schindler, who started to be complicit. He profited from war, mingling with power. But something shifted. He saw enough. Asked enough. And the asking changed him. What began as survival slowly turned into resistance. He chose to save lives. Not out of moral perfection, but because the questions became too loud to silence.

And what about the everyday truths … the small ones we warp without noticing? Saying you're fine when you're not. Smiling when you're furious. Apologising when you don't mean it, or withholding one when you should. We curate our truths in service of peace, or politeness, or self-protection. But do we ever stop to ask: *What cost are we paying?*

So maybe integrity isn't about being right all the time. Maybe it's about being honest with yourself in real time.

About asking:

Who benefits?

Who breaks?

What truth am I holding on to, and why?

And also:

Which truth am I avoiding, and how long can I keep pretending not to see it?

And in that asking, we're reshaped. Not into saints. Not into heroes. But into people who are awake to the weight of what it means to choose.

In the end, integrity may not be a possession. It may be a path. Winding, imperfect, and full of pauses. We don't change when answers arrive. We change in the quiet act of wondering what we've always assumed to be true.

In the asking, I changed.

And maybe that's the point.

Lost Conversations

When did we start fearing silence more than meaningless talk?

When did the pause between words become a threat rather than a doorway?

When did quiet begin to feel like a void we must hurry to fill with trivia, opinions, or the next punchline?

What small, cumulative changes turned restive silence… once the soil of reflection … into a discomfort we will endlessly anaesthetize?

I sometimes went to a nearby café to work, and one day I noticed something. Not the grand gestures, but the micro-movements.

Two people who once talked for hours now sit with their cups cooling between them, the steam thinning into nothing. Their thumbs move across glowing screens, faces lit by a light too blue to feel human. The background music hums like a polite intruder, smoothing over any trace of awkwardness. A group of friends nearby laugh in short, bright bursts, their laughter rising and falling in rhythm with notifications. Their table glows … half-empty cups, half-finished thoughts, the scent of espresso now dull in the air. Somewhere, a spoon taps against porcelain, marking the seconds between words that no one speaks.

Even in offices, silence has become suspect. Meetings pulse with overlapping voices, the soft clack of keys, the whir of machines. The pauses … once used to think … are now treated like inefficiency. People fill them quickly with affirmations and buzzwords. "*Got it.*" "*Exactly.*" "*Next slide.*" The air hums with busyness, but meaning thins out like air in a crowded elevator. The rhythm of productivity has become our new conversation partner.

Why do we treat silence as a danger? What are we running from when we fill the air so quickly?

It isn't silence we fear … it's what waits inside it.

Am I enough? Do I matter?

What if there's nothing underneath the noise? Those questions hover quietly like dust in sunlight. We prefer movement, distraction, anything that keeps us from meeting them.

Once, silence was a teacher.

In ancient symposiums, philosophers let pauses ferment between ideas, giving thought time to ripen.

In monasteries, silence is a doorway to God, not an absence of Him.

In Japanese tea ceremonies, silence itself became etiquette, a shared reverence that needed no words.

Even in ordinary homes, silence had its own hours…the hush after dinner, the moment before sleep, the sound of a turning page. We lived among pauses, not against them.

Then the rhythm changed. The industrial clock began to tick, and silence became "*unproductive.*" Machines filled the stillness with hums and bells. Radios arrived to narrate the day; televisions to narrate the night. When the internet came, it filled the spaces between both. Even solitude was colonised… first by background music, then by the endless feed of *"new."*

We began to mistake constant connection for meaning. We replaced presence with visibility, reflection with commentary. Even grief now asks for captions.

Anthropologists call small, shallow talk phatic communication … speech that says, *"I'm here." "You're here." "We still exist."* It's essential. Without it, society would collapse under cold efficiency. But when phatic talk becomes the only language we speak, depth decays.

What happens when "*How are you?*" becomes a reflex, not a bridge? When does the word "*fine*" become armour rather than truth? When our conversations sound like rehearsals for empathy but never quite reach it?

Technology is not the villain, but it's an accomplice. Notifications are sugar … short, sweet, addictive. We check messages mid-sentence, mid-meal, mid-thought. The phone resting on the table becomes a third guest, silent but insistent. You can feel it change the air. The speaker's eyes dart, the listener's tone shifts, the pulse of conversation loses depth. Even silence becomes performative … we scroll while we pause, as if stillness needs to multitask.

What does this do to us, year after year?

It weakens the muscle of listening. It makes stillness feel like absence instead of presence. We mistake conversation for connection and noise for proof of life.

We are surrounded by words but starving for understanding.

Step into a train at rush hour. Every seat glows with a small blue light. The carriage hums, not with talk, but with the faint buzz of headphones leaking different worlds … music, news, reels, voices that don't belong to anyone nearby. We share space, but not silence. Our quiet is crowded with digital ghosts.

At night, cities hum with artificial life. You can hear it if you stand by an open window … the distant whir of engines, a car horn dissolving into the distance, a television flickering through paper-thin walls.

In that soft cacophony, we call it white noise to make it sound harmless. But perhaps that's the problem … our noise has learned how to disguise itself as comfort.

Even homes hum differently now. The faint buzz of chargers, the glow of standby lights, the whisper of constant connectivity. Silence no longer feels natural; it feels extinct.

What are we afraid might happen if we turned everything off?

Silence doesn't just unsettle us … it exposes us. In its space, we meet the things we edit out. Loneliness, grief, longing, fatigue, questions without answers. It's easier to talk than to feel. Easier to fill the air than to let our own voice tremble in it.

But perhaps trembling is part of being alive.

A friend once told me that when her father died, she couldn't bear the silence at home. She kept the television on, even while sleeping. "*It made me feel less alone*," she said. "*Until one day, I turned it off. The quiet was unbearable ... but it was also the first time I felt him near.*"

Silence doesn't erase what we love; it lets us hear it differently.

We often forget that silence isn't one thing. There's the heavy silence of absence. The awkward silence of uncertainty. The sacred silence of attention. The restorative silence of rest. The companionable silence that hums between people who trust each other. They all sound different if you listen long enough.

What kind of silence are you avoiding today?

Sometimes, silence is not emptiness … it's incubation. The Japanese call it *ma* … the pause that gives shape to sound. Without *ma*, music collapses into chaos. Without quiet, words lose weight. The space between things gives them meaning.

Think of a child learning to speak. There's always a pause before the next word … a small, brave silence as language forms. Or lovers in mid-argument, suddenly quiet, realising that silence might save them more than another sentence would. Silence is the breath that makes creation possible.

In a world obsessed with immediacy, silence feels like rebellion.

We rush to reply, to react, to fill. But deep talk asks for delay … for the patience to let meaning settle. The philosopher's pause was once a mark of respect; now it's treated as hesitation. But maybe we need that hesitation. It's where truth takes its first breath.

Our childhoods were once threaded with silence … the slow rhythm of afternoons without screens, the hum of ceiling fans, the distant sounds of life outside. We filled time with imagination, not notifications. The silence of boredom taught us how to make worlds. Now, boredom terrifies us. We've forgotten that boredom was the womb of creativity.

When did quiet stop being fertile and start feeling fatal?

I remember a night on a train when two strangers began to talk. The carriage swayed softly; outside, the darkness passed like water. Their voices were low, hesitant at first, then open. They spoke about loss, about feeling invisible, about starting over. Between their words, there were long pauses … the kind of pauses that only exist when people are listening, not performing. When the train stopped, they didn't exchange names. They simply nodded, as if silence itself had introduced them.

We underestimate how much a slow connection can hold.

In a relationship, silence is the space where trust matures. Between friends, it's the comfort that no explanation is needed. Within ourselves, it's the mirror that shows what noise hides.

Perhaps we have confused emptiness with depth. We fill every pause because we think silence means something is missing, when often it means something real is forming.

Even the brain needs silence. Studies show that moments of stillness help integrate memory and emotion, allowing creativity to surface.

The mind, like a lake, reflects best when it's undisturbed.

What would our world look like if we treated silence as essential maintenance for the mind?

Imagine schools that taught listening as literacy. Meetings that began with a minute of quiet before speaking. Workplaces that reward reflection as much as response. Public spaces where phones were off not by rule, but by choice. A culture that praised reflection as much as expression.

We might become slower, yes … but also gentler.

Because silence softens us. It lets empathy return. It reminds us that we don't have to respond to everything immediately, or at all. It permits to feel before we speak.

At dusk, when the city quiets for a few brief minutes before night takes over, there's a moment when sound changes texture. You can hear footsteps echo differently. A single voice carries farther. The wind hums through electric wires.

That's the sound of collective exhale … the world remembering itself.

We could learn from that.

Silence doesn't need to be earned. It only needs to be noticed.

Start small. Turn off the background noise. Sit with someone without rushing to fill the space. Let your thoughts arrive late, unpolished.

Ask questions that take time to answer:

"What are you missing lately?"

"What hasn't been said?"

Let the pauses do some of the talking.

When you listen long enough, silence reveals its personality … textured, alive, full of quiet choreography. It's not a void. It's a landscape. The rustle of leaves, the clink of a spoon, the faint buzz of a streetlamp … all of it belongs to the language of stillness.

We spend so much time fearing the absence of sound that we forget how full silence really is.

It is not the enemy of connection but its anchor. Not an interruption, but an interval. Not the death of meaning, but its birthplace.

Perhaps the truest measure of connection isn't how much we say, but how much we can share without words.

So next time a conversation falters, don't rescue it. Let it breathe. Watch what happens when you trust the pause.

The hum of the café. The hush before confession. The stillness between laughter. The gentle silence of early morning before alarms break the spell. The quiet that follows forgiveness. These are not empty moments; they are the architecture of being human.

When we lose silence, we also lose the depth that makes conversation worthwhile. Without stillness, our words skim the surface of living; we speak to respond, not to relate.

But real conversation … the kind that unfolds slowly, that bends and deepens with thought … is one of the few remaining ways humans remember how to think together.

We are not meant to exist in monologues. The mind, left unchallenged, turns inward until its ideas circle themselves. It's through dialogue that we stretch. A good conversation doesn't simply exchange words; it expands the boundaries of what each person believed was true. To speak with depth is to offer your mind to be reshaped.

Every culture that thrived intellectually or spiritually … from the ancient Greek agora to the Sufi gatherings, from Enlightenment salons to small-town courtyards … understood that collective thought keeps the human spirit elastic.

People gathered to discuss philosophy, art, grief, politics, and poetry. They questioned, disagreed, and built upon one another's words. Conversation was not decoration; it was oxygen.

Now we inhale headlines instead of ideas. We confuse opinion with understanding. We talk faster, but say less. The art of discourse…once an act of trust and curiosity…has become a performance of certainty.

We debate to win, not to grow. We listen to reply, not to hear. And in doing so, we lose the quiet alchemy that turns dialogue into discovery.

But we need those kinds of conversations…the ones that make us slower, more alert, more alive. Conversations where silence sits comfortably between thoughts, where people reach for meaning instead of dominance. Without them, imagination dries up. Empathy becomes mechanical.

Communities fracture not because people disagree, but because they've forgotten how to stay curious while doing so.

Meaningful talk teaches us patience. It reminds us that not every question has an immediate answer, and not every difference is a threat. It gives us the chance to see another person's logic without needing to erase our own. It allows complexity … that rare thing modern life tries so hard to flatten.

Perhaps that's why so many of us feel unseen even in company.

We're surrounded by dialogue, yet starving for conversation. The kind that makes your mind hum hours later. The kind that changes your posture, because you leave it lighter or heavier in the right way. The kind that rearranges something subtle in you … the moral, emotional, or intellectual furniture of your being.

To have more of these, we must first slow down. Good conversation doesn't bloom in haste. It needs time, presence, and the courage to be unfinished.

It needs the humility to ask questions that might not make us look clever, but make us more human.

Ask:

What really matters to you lately?

What have you changed your mind about?

What truth do you hesitate to say aloud?

These are not big questions … they are doorways. Through them, people return to themselves.

Our world is saturated with speech but starved of exchange. And yet, a single real conversation can repair more loneliness than a hundred digital notifications. Because what we crave isn't noise … it's recognition. We don't need to agree with; we need to be understood.

When we gather to think, wonder, or ache together, we participate in something ancient … the slow restoration of meaning. Each good conversation becomes a quiet protest against a culture that values reaction over reflection.

If we are to reclaim the depth of our humanity, we must learn again to sit with each other in the long, unhurried rhythm of words and silence.

To bring our curiosity to the table like an offering.

To let ideas take their time. To speak not to perform, but to connect.

Because to speak deeply is not just to share … it is to remember.

To converse meaningfully is to rebuild the fragile architecture of understanding itself.

In the asking, I changed.

And in listening for what mattered, I found that silence was not an ending … it was the language we had forgotten to remember.

Rims of Respect

What are boundaries, really?

Are they fences, permissions, quiet chalk lines around our lives?

Or are they something softer, like whispered prayers, not *"stay away,"* but *"see me gently"*? Not walls, but thresholds, invitations to approach with care.

We often imagine boundaries as confrontational, declarations made with a hard voice and braced shoulders.

But maybe boundaries were never about pushing other people out.

Maybe they are how we stay in touch with ourselves, the small rituals by which we honour our inner weather. Maybe they are not shields, but ways of staying present without abandoning who we are.

So why does naming them feel like such a trembling thing?

There is a strange intimacy in speaking a limit aloud. The word feels fragile in the mouth, almost apologetic, while the act it represents sometimes requires a courage that startles us with its sharpness.

A boundary asks you to hold two truths at once: that you are soft, and also that you will not be flattened. It asks you to let language carry a private geography, a quiet map of what hurts and what matters.

But naming discomfort feels risky, so we learn detours instead. We change the subject. We laugh. We say *"It's fine"* when something inside us knows it isn't. We swallow discomfort to protect the atmosphere, to avoid rearranging the room.

Shrinking can feel safer than speaking.

Naming a boundary feels like making an accusation, even when it is simply an act of honesty. Yet honesty is often the very thing we have been taught to ration.

A friend once called me while walking home from dinner. I could hear her keys as she let herself into her apartment, the soft echo of her feet on the floor. She had just come from a gathering where an old friend leaned too close again, commented on her love life again, and held her arm a moment too long after she gently pulled away.

She stood in front of her bathroom mirror later, lipstick still perfect, but her heartbeat felt unsettled.

"Was I overreacting?" she asked, brushing imaginary lint from her sleeve.

Why is it so easy to doubt our own discomfort?

It is often the smallest domestic details that carry the weight, the cold of the doorknob, the faint smell of spices still clinging to her jacket, the lipstick mark on the glass that remained exactly where she left it.

These textures reveal a boundary long before the words do. The body knows something is wrong before the mind finds language.

The body always notices first. Shoulders that do not fully settle. A tightening at the sternum. The breath becomes shallow. The script of explanations you prepare before anyone even asks.

We become fluent in convincing ourselves that the discomfort is our fault. "Was I overreacting?" becomes the opening line of a negotiation with your own truth.

But what does it take to say calmly, *"That is too close"*?

What if we were raised to make others comfortable before we learned to protect ourselves?

Every family, every culture, offers its own choreography of belonging. Some teach respect. Some teach silence. Some teach that love must be proven by endurance. And some teach disappearance.

If your childhood lessons placed more weight on avoiding offence than naming what hurts, the muscles for boundary-setting will feel shaky, tender, and a little unfamiliar.

A lifetime of smoothing your own edges does not make you kinder. It makes you quieter. To learn to voice a need is to relearn how to live in your own body with permission.

Boundaries are the soft outlines of our selfhood. They define what feels safe, what feels sacred. There are quiet agreements we make about what we can carry and what we must set down.

Soft outlines do not mean soft consequences. Limits protect the interior. They are the hidden stitching that gives our shape strength.

To set a boundary is not to isolate. It is to shape how you will show up, so your presence is sustainable. Boundaries are not refusals. They are agreements of care, both for yourself and for the relationship.

But why do so many people hear them as abandonment?

Perhaps because our stories often teach that closeness means access. If love equals availability, if friendship means instant response, if affection means uninterrupted access to your energy, then "no" sounds like rejection.

Many of us learned that saying no was a rupture rather than a rhythm.

I once knew a woman who had a close friend she cherished. They shared years of playlists and midnight conversations, stitched together by mutual loneliness. But slowly, his messages grew frequent, expectant. He grew cold when she replied too slowly. Twice, when she cancelled dinner, he showed up anyway. She learned to laugh lightly to ease his disappointment. But her stomach tightened every time her phone buzzed.

When she finally said, *"I need space,"* he called her *Selfish. Dramatic. Unkind.*

There is a particular sorrow in being treated as a resource someone believes they are owed. What once felt affectionate begins to feel heavy. Her polite smile became a mask she wore for survival. Naming her boundary was not rejection. It was self-preservation.

How do you tell someone that needing space is not the same as walking away?

Sometimes, you cannot.

Sometimes the work is simply to repeat your truth, calmly, without apology.

"I need space" is not a negotiation. It is a fact.

Explanations invite argument. Clarity ends it.

But boundaries are not only for those outside us. Some of the hardest boundaries are with ourselves.

How often do we push beyond exhaustion because productivity feels easier than rest? How often do we criticise ourselves for wanting quiet? How often do we abandon our own needs to keep moving, as if motion could replace meaning?

There is a quiet boundary that says, *"I will no longer speak to myself with cruelty."*

Another that says, *"I will rest before I collapse."*

Another that says, *"I do not need to earn joy."*

Boundaries with ourselves are often the most radical, because they ask us to rewrite the very way we understand worth.

What if setting a boundary with the self is not a form of discipline, but a form of tenderness? What would life look like if you believed that what you need does not disqualify you from love?

Digital life complicates this further. Notifications pull us across invisible lines all day. Every buzz suggests urgency. Every unread message asks for our attention. And attention starts to feel like currency.

We begin to answer before we think. We reply before we know how we feel. Our boundaries soften into availability.

Our phones become small doors we forget how to close.

What if logging out was not avoidance, but care? What if silence online could be seen as presence elsewhere?

Many people now feel guilt for not sharing pain quickly enough, as though a boundary around grief requires explanation. But maybe some chapters of our lives are meant to be lived before they are told. Not because we are hiding. But healing often begins without witnesses.

Sometimes silence itself is a boundary. Not the kind that pushes others away, but the kind that protects our becoming. Silence can be a pocket of safety. A room where the self can stretch.

What if silence were seen not as secrecy, but sacred space?

One of my closest friends was entering the dating world again. She was beginning to go on dates after years of heartbreak. She loved slowly. She asked gentle questions. But each time something felt wrong, her words tangled in apology. She feared seeming difficult. She wanted to be chosen more than she wanted to be respected. And one night, after feeling brushed aside during a conversation, I finally asked her, *"Do you want closeness, or do you want kindness?"*

Sometimes the boundary arrives as a question. Sometimes that question is enough to change everything.

We speak often about permission. But perhaps the deeper question is: Where did we learn we must earn it? Are boundaries only allowed when others approve? Or do they come alive the moment we believe ourselves worthy of having them?

Boundaries, when seen correctly, are not about control. They are about rhythm. They teach us how to be present without being depleted. They allow connection without collapse. They remind us that love does not require endless stretching, but honest shape.

But this understanding is not simple. It involves unlearning. Practice. And a willingness to be misunderstood.

She was sitting across from her mother at the kitchen table, tea cooling quietly. The same conversation unfolded: her choices, her job, her clothes. Each sentence shaped like care, each one heavy.

She stirred her cup and said, softly, *"Can we not talk about that today?"* Her mother frowned. *"You have become so sensitive."*

Why is sensitivity the accusation we use when someone finally says, "This hurts"?

Families operate through unspoken patterns. A mother's worry can be love tangled with expectation. Asking for a pause is not ingratitude. It is simply a request for breath. Naming hurt is not a disruption. It is clarity. But clarity is not always welcome.

Culture complicates this further. We speak of harmony, but confuse it with silence. We speak of respect, but sometimes mean obedience. Yet boundaries, when seen truly, protect harmony because they prevent resentment from growing quietly in the dark.

Sometimes the hardest boundaries are with those who love us deeply, because their stories about us were written long before we learned to speak.

And then there is the workplace, where no one teaches you how to guard your edges. Late-night messages disguised as opportunity, team bonding disguised as emotional labour, personal questions disguised as kindness.

Your time slowly becomes communal. Your energy becomes assumed. Until you realise that saying yes was never a paid part of your role.

One day, I said no.

I skipped the after-hours call.

I did not justify.

I did not apologise.

And the next morning, someone whispered, *"Not a team player."*

Why does asserting yourself make people uncomfortable?

Because so much of politeness is built on quiet compliance.

One no reveals a truth everyone was pretending not to see, that your labour, your time, your body, were never owed.

Perhaps the problem is not misunderstanding. Perhaps some people simply dislike the inconvenience of adjusting to your humanity.

But no is not cruelty.

No is clarity.

And sometimes, no is the first yes you give to yourself.

There is a liberation in drawing a line that returns you to your own life. Saying yes to yourself is not selfish. It is the condition that allows generosity to be real and not performed.

Attachment theory tells us that early relationships shape our sense of safety. If we grew up fearing that displeasing someone meant losing them, even the quietest boundary feels like danger.

"I don't like that" begins to sound like *"please don't abandon me."*

We learn to fear our own needs because they might cost us love.

Unlearning that takes time.

Gentleness.

And repetition.

You rehearse small sentences.

You test tiny limits.

You notice the world does not collapse.

You find people who respond with kindness.

You let yourself be awkward because awkwardness means something new is being written.

What would life feel like if children were taught that their time was their own, their bodies were their own, and their silence was their own?

What would our homes look like if "*no*" were treated with acceptance instead of judgment? What kind of adults would we become if we learned that protecting our energy was not rebellion, but responsibility?

Boundaries are not only personal. They are cultural. They are systemic. Some people's limits are respected immediately. Others must fight for basic validation. Some people are allowed to be fatigue. Others are expected to outlast it.

I was once the only junior member on the team and the only woman, too. My boss called me "kiddo", even in meetings. I smiled tightly. I took on extra tasks. I skipped lunch most days. It took me months to realise that no one had ever asked what my actual role was. They assumed, and I adapted.

So, I redrew the lines.

Slowly.

I refused midnight messages.

I spoke up during meetings.

I removed "kiddo" from my vocabulary, even if others didn't.

It was not aggression.

It was visibility.

The gentle insistence on being seen as whole.

How do we teach the world to ask for access instead of assuming it?

We model it with small acts.

We thank people when they ask.

We build systems where consent becomes as ordinary as breathing, where presence is not mistaken for permission.

How do we stay soft while still protecting ourselves?

By recognising that softness is not the absence of limits. It is the reason limits exist. Softness must be guarded if it is to survive. A tender person can be resolute. It is possible to care deeply and still say no.

Boundaries are not the end of love.

They are how love lasts.

They are not walls. They are doors with locks and handles. They say, "You are welcome here, but only if you knock."

And on the days, someone walks in without knocking, what then?

You close the door.

You lock it.

And you remember, you are allowed to do so.

In the asking, I changed.

And I chose myself without explanation.

Emotional Debt We Don't Count

We say it like a reflex. A breath, a bullet: "I'm fine."

It slides between people the way a coin slides across a table … small, smooth, easy to ignore.

We use it to close a conversation, to keep the line from cracking, to avoid the tremor in our own voice that asks too many questions.

We rehearse it in mirrors, in bathrooms, in tiny rehearsals before calls: the polite lie that keeps the world manageable.

But what happens when those small, almost-invisible fibs begin to add up? What is the ledger of quiet denials that we carry in our chests?

The metaphor of debt is not accidental. Debt accrues interest. It does not demand attention until it does … until the bill arrives in a way that cannot be deferred.

Each "I'm fine" when it is not is a micro-credit borrowed from someone's understanding and returned later with interest in the form of distance, misunderstanding, and internal corrosion. The price is not always immediate.

More often, it compounds; a feeling left unspoken today hardens into a pattern tomorrow; a withheld truth becomes an armour that also keeps out warmth.

Why do we prefer the small tidy lie?

Part of it is kindness in a social language that prizes smoothness. We learn early that conflict is dangerous; we learn that emotional honesty requires bravery and sometimes invites chaos.

Politeness Theory, explored by Brown and Levinson, suggests we manage each other's "face"…the social value we project … by softening potential threats. "I'm fine" is often a face-saving phrase. It preserves the other's comfort and our role as compliant, non-burdensome citizens. But politeness also has a cost.

Who bears it?

Emotional labour, the phrase Arlie Hochschild coined for the work of managing feelings to fit a role, sits at the heart of this habit. Some of us are paid to smile, to reassure, to be unflappable.

Others are socialised into the unpaid labour of calming rooms, smoothing conversations, and refusing to be too much.

Women, in particular, are often trained into a soft economy of emotional generosity: you soothe the meeting, diffuse the argument, reassure the anxious colleague, and say you're fine while pieces of you pile up in corners.

What does it do to be a perpetual caretaker of comfort that does not return the favour?

There are practical reasons we say "I'm fine" instead of the strung-out truth.

Vulnerability scares us because it makes us unpredictable to others and ourselves. Confessing "I'm exhausted" might invite questions you cannot answer. Saying "I'm overwhelmed" might trigger a reassignment of blame. Declaring "I'm not okay" can feel like opening a door to an emotional room you cannot afford to inhabit when emails pile up, and children need food and bills need paying.

We hide behind the phrase because the world sometimes requires us to keep functioning regardless of internal weather.

But the accumulation of tiny untruths changes us. It rewires patterns of intimacy. When someone hears "I'm fine" enough times, the phrase loses meaning; it becomes a default signal rather than information.

The listener stops asking because they assume the speaker is rehearsing a standard response. The speaker, seeing the lack of curiosity, feels unseen, so the next time they practice the same small concealment.

It is a feedback loop that erodes trust more effectively than any single betrayal. How many relationships have been softened out of existence by rehearsed politeness?

Think, for a moment, of a marriage in which one partner says "I'm fine" every night for months. The other partner hears it, nods, and goes to bed. After a while, the partner who hears begins to assume "fine" is a category of completeness: no room for follow-up, no flag. The speaker begins to believe their feelings are invisible even to themselves, because no one has listened long enough to reflect them. The consequence is not only lonely hearts … it is the slow cultural extinction of curiosity between two people who once vowed to know each other.

The body also keeps score. Suppressed feelings do not evaporate. They find expression in headaches, stomach aches, insomnia, and clenched jaws.

Somatic psychologists remind us that emotions are embodied before they are articulated.

A chest that tightens when a conversation veers close to the truth is evidence of a body holding a ledger. Emotional debt is a physiological state as well as a relational one. Have you noticed how the days when you insist you are "fine" often leave you physically drained, as if the act of lying were itself a kind of drain on energy?

There are also social dynamics at play. We live in a culture that privileges stoicism in many forms: "Keep calm and carry on" has been translated into a thousand different professional and private idioms.

Men, across many societies, are often taught to answer vulnerability with denial; their "I'm fine" becomes armour in a world that punishes visible fragility.

For others, the denial is a survival strategy in workplaces that penalise emotional bandwidth.

A teacher who says "I'm fine" when they are overwhelmed avoids administrative scrutiny but eats the stress quietly. What does it cost to protect an institution, a role, or an image more than our own inner life?

And then there is the politics of visibility. Some identities … race, class, gender, disability … shape whether it feels safe to say "I'm not fine."

Marginalised people often learn that voicing pain invites dismissal or backlash. Saying you are struggling can be read as weakness or as an invitation for extra scrutiny. In those contexts, "I'm fine" is a protective stance that says: I will not give you the ammunition to question my competence, my loyalty, my right to be present. The calculus is chilling: honesty can be costly. What would change if our institutions made it safer to reveal our interior weather?

The presumptive civility of "I'm fine" also masks a poverty of language. We are under-taught in how to articulate complex moods.

Saying "I'm not okay, but I don't want advice" is a nuanced sentence that requires both speaker and listener to hold multiple truths: that vulnerability can exist without fix-it impulses, that comfort does not require problem solving.

Our conversational toolkit is impoverished: we collapse into "fine" because we lack the words, the permission, or the practice to say otherwise.

How often have you wished you had a phrase in your pocket that conveyed "I'm frayed, but I can still meet you for tea if you'll just listen"?

There's also the danger of emotional outsourcing. Saying "I'm fine" can be a way of passing the responsibility for the feeling back to yourself: You will carry it alone.

Over time, the habit of solitary containment can harden into isolation. You may think you are being considerate by not dumping, but you are also starving your relationships of vivid truth. A friend who never hears the real weather cannot practice the art of empathic presence. How, then, do we train the muscles of mutuality if we never allow them to flex?

Small lies have ripple effects beyond the individual.

I remember working in a team that normalised "I'm fine" when individuals were strained fostering burnout. Projects succeeded at the cost of human fatigue.

In families, children learn to mask their inner state and carry a template of stoicism into adulthood. Societies that value constant competence over reflective care craft citizens who are less likely to ask for help and more likely to suffer silently.

What public policies … mental health days, mandatory check-ins, culture shifts … would reduce the necessity of defaulting to "fine"?

Yet, despite the harm, there are ways to interrupt the debt cycle. Interruption begins with naming the economy in which the lie circulates: calling it "emotional debt" gives it weight and legitimacy. Once named, we can begin experiments. The practice of small, truthful disclosures is one route: not oversharing, but practising micro-honesty.

Try the simple substitution test: instead of "I'm fine," say *"A little tired," "Not great today,"* or

"I'm dealing with something." These phrases are neither pleas nor full narratives; they are honest calibrations that invite a low-cost response. They also retrain the listener to ask follow-up questions over time.

Another practice is the explicit boundary. You might say, *"I'm not great, but I don't want advice... can you just sit with me for five minutes?"* or *"I'm feeling uneasy; could we postpone this conversation until I've had time to think?"* These are small acts of communication that preserve dignity and ask for care without demanding over-involvement. They teach others how to hold you and teach you how to ask for what you need.

Rituals matter too. In some families and workplaces, a simple check-in can change the culture: one minute at the start of a meeting where each person names their emotional weather. Not a confessional, but a status report. Over time, it builds a muscle for honesty and reduces the pressure to perform normalcy. Try it in a small group and watch the difference. The aim is not therapeutic oversharing but human calibration: we are all carrying weather, and a little acknowledgement can change the climate.

There are practices of repair for the debt already accrued. If you notice you have been saying "I'm fine" to someone important, there is a repair script that is both simple and brave: *"I want to be honest.*

I've been saying I'm fine when I haven't been. I didn't want to burden you, but that was my mistake. I'm having a hard time." Apologising for withholding is not weakness; it is an admission that the relationship matters and that you are invested in its integrity. How many relationships can be saved by a quiet repair like that?

Teaching better language for feelings is also an act of generosity. We can model sentences that are brief and specific: *"I'm overwhelmed today"* is stronger than "I'm fine" and more usable than an indefinite complaint.

Language like *"I'm lonely"* or *"I'm anxious about tomorrow"* gives others something to anchor to. It turns emotional interiority into a shared object rather than an opaque weight. How would your conversations change if you taught the people around you a few clear phrases?

There are therapeutic and communal resources as well. Group therapy, peer support, or a friend-check system can take pressure off single relationships. If you have one person with whom you can practice truth, that one practice ripples outward.

Some people create a "truth buddy," someone who is safe to tell the small things: *"I'm not fine today"* becomes an expected line rather than a betrayal. What would it feel like to name one person as your repository for honest check-ins?

There are cultural shifts to be advocated. Workplaces can normalise mental health days, leaders can model micro-vulnerability (saying *"I'm tired today"* without penalty), and public conversation can make space for the incomplete phrase: *"I'm managing"* or *"I'm coping imperfectly."*

We admire stoicism, but what if we admired courage to see and name truth? A society that normalises small, real confessions builds citizens who are easier to be with.

We must also be compassionate with ourselves. The habit of saying "I'm fine" is often adaptive. It protected you in specific contexts. It may have saved a career, a family dinner, a reputation.

Rewiring is slow and requires forgiveness for past strategies that once served you.

Start with curiosity:

Where did the lie originate?

Who rewarded it?

Which bodies taught it to you?

When you answer these, you will see the pattern less as a moral failing and more as an artefact of survival.

Ask yourself:

Where have I spent my emotional currency?

Who am I protecting when I say "I'm fine"?

What would happen if I were honest for one conversation this week?

Who would I trust?

What would it feel like to carry less debt in my chest?

And then, ask the reciprocal question:

When someone says "I'm fine," what do you do?

Do you let it slide?

Do you ask gently, "Are you sure?"

Do you learn the quiet art of tracking the small telltales…a voice that tightens, a laugh that lands wrong, eyes that dart away?

Being the person who notices is a discipline. You do not need to fix, only to attend. Sometimes the most generous response to "I'm fine" is the offer: *"Okay. I'm here if you want to talk,"* or the simple silence that says, I will hold this.

We will have days when "I'm fine" is true. That phrase will continue to be useful. The aim is not to eradicate it but to remove its tyranny … so that it is an accurate status rather than a universal reflex.

The goal is to owe less to ourselves and others in small unspoken ways, to close the emotional accounts we carry so they do not compound into overwhelm.

If you feel the weight of small lies, consider a modest experiment: for one week, replace "I'm fine" with a truthful, short sentence … *"I'm tired," "I'm sad," "I'm okay, but today is hard."* Notice the micro-reactions in others. Notice the release in yourself. It might be small at first, awkward, even embarrassing. Then watch the ledger open and the interest decline.

Emotional debt accrues quietly. It is repaid in distance, in aches, in the slow erosion of what it means to be seen. The currency of truth is small but compoundingly valuable: a single honest sentence can be paid forward into a cascade of care.

So, what will you say the next time you are asked how you are? Will you hand over another coin, smooth and small and false, or will you risk a sentence that requires nothing dramatic but could rewire what you owe?

If you choose the latter, you begin to close the accounts that have been accumulating far too long.

And that closure will feel like a small, restored credit … less debt, more daylight.

In the asking, I changed.

And the weight I put down was one I didn't know I was carrying.

Self-Forgiveness

What does it mean to forgive yourself?

Is it the same act as forgiving someone else … a tidy release, a handshake, a closing of the book … or something lonelier, messier, and quieter?

Why do we imagine self-forgiveness as a single clean moment when it so often looks like long, unseen labour? What makes us so uncomfortable with slow repair? Why do we distrust processes we cannot see finishing neatly?

Who taught us that forgiveness must be magnanimous and instantaneous, rather than patient and slow? And why does that expectation leave so many of us feeling stuck, as if mercy were a commodity we somehow failed to earn?

We speak easily of forgiving others … after an argument, a betrayal, a mistake … because the script exists: apology, contrition, pardon, reconciliation.

But forgiving ourselves has no standardised ritual. There is no social liturgy to officiate it. The internal script is fragmentary: we tell ourselves to “move on,” to “let it go,” and when we don’t, we conclude we are stubbornly broken.

Why do we expect the same economy of closure inwardly that the world grants outwardly? Who benefits from that expectation? And who quietly suffers under it?

The unseen challenges to forgiving ourselves begin in language and culture. Shame and guilt live in the same neighbourhood but behave differently: guilt says, *“I did something bad,”* shame says, *“I am bad.”* Which one lives in your chest? How would your life change if you could tell the difference more clearly? What if you stopped punishing yourself for what shame, not guilt, is carrying?

Guilt can be reparable; shame corrodes identity. We are taught to atone for the former and to hide the latter. When the moral ledger is fuzzy … when consequences were complex, intentions tangled, outcomes harmful despite good intent … how do you account for yourself fairly? How do you balance responsibility with mercy? Is mercy something you believe must be earned? Or something that allows responsibility to be borne without collapse?

One of my colleagues is a mother who once raised her voice at her teenager and still, years later, wakes at 3 a.m. with the memory like a small stone in her throat. She told me one day when I asked her if she didn't get enough sleep.

The apology was offered, hugs exchanged, the pattern changed, but the memory lingers and morphs into a narrative: *"I am a bad mother."* She repeats the ledger of transgressions to herself like a prayer. Forgiving herself would require her to see the situation differently: that a single harsh moment does not define a full life of care.

Why do singular moments gain so much authority in our self-narratives? Who taught us that a mistake deserves lifelong narration?

But how do you rewrite a habit of self-censure? What practices would you need to teach a heart that keeps tally?

One of my friends, an entrepreneur. His startup failed after two years of garbage-bag sleeping in incubators and relentless pitching. Investors left, staff scattered, and now, months later, each notification feels like an indictment.

He knows intellectually that failure is common; he reads books about pivoting, resilience, and growth. But there is an inner judge that counts wasted time as moral failure, not as learning.

How do you make space for mercy when your livelihood and identity once rode on a venture that didn't survive? How do you neutralise the narrative that equates collapse with worthlessness? What parts of yourself did you tie too tightly to success? What would remain if you loosened that knot?

Some survivors lived through an accident and carry guilt for being alive when others did not. Survivors' guilt is a heavy and paradoxical burden; gratitude for breath tangled with a persistent sense of having taken what wasn't strictly yours. Forgiving yourself here is not forgiving a direct wrongdoing; it is forgiving the arbitrary geography of fate.

How do you answer a heart that insists on fairness where none exists? Is fairness the same as justice? Or is it sometimes a longing for control dressed as morality?

These are not rare cases. Every day life furnishes small and large ways we withhold forgiveness.

The friend who cut you off for words said in pain.

The student who plagiarised once was out of panic.

The caregiver who snapped after months of no sleep.

The common thread is that self-forgiveness is complicated by context, by the fear that forgiving yourself is letting yourself off the hook, by the worry that mercy will encourage repetition.

How do you ensure forgiveness does not become a license for the same harm? What does accountability look like when it is quiet and ongoing? Who are you becoming through that work?

Philosophers and therapists offer maps but not easy roads.

Stoics invite us to accept what we cannot change and to pursue the only agency we have: how we act now.

Buddhists teach non-attachment and compassion toward suffering as the path to end it.

Psychologists like Kristin Neff frame self-compassion as a three-part practice: self-kindness, recognition of shared humanity, and mindful acceptance.

But knowledge and practice are not the same. Why does knowing the right thing to do feel insufficient in the middle of shame's fog? What part of you resists instruction but longs for presence? What kind of knowing lives outside logic?

Part of the difficulty is embodiment. Emotions are not only narratives; they are muscle and breath and bone. Shame lives in posture: a rounded back, downward glance, the feeling of a weight on the sternum.

Treatments that target cognition without addressing the body can fall short.

How do you teach the body new ways to hold itself when the old shape has been learned through years of worry? Can you breathe into that knot and persuade the muscles that safety exists? What would safety feel like in your body right now? When was the last time your body felt believed?

Practical work helps. The first unseen step is naming. Before you can forgive, you must bring the wrong to language: what happened, what was your role, what harm did you cause, what harm was outside your control? Naming turns a ghost into a thing you can work with. It also helps to distinguish responsibility from identity: I did X versus I am X. Which sentence can you practice this week? Can you make a small journal entry that starts, "I did…" rather than "I am …" and notice how it shifts the tone?

Repair, where possible, is also important. Self-forgiveness is not an excuse to avoid restitution. If you can make amends, do so. If you cannot, find other forms of reparation: volunteer service, a concrete project that uses your skills for good, or making a ritual offering. Sometimes reparation is impossible … you cannot unhurt the dead … but symbolically repairing can alter the internal atmosphere.

What small act would feel like a real attempt at balance? Who are you trying to convince with that act, others or yourself? What would sincerity look like here?

Then there is the ritual of witnesses. We are social animals; being seen matters.

Confession … not in the punitive religious sense but as vocalising truth to a trusted other … can break shame's monopoly. A single person who hears your account without condemnation can be medicine. Therapy is one such model, but friendship, mentorship, or group rituals can also be witnessed.

Who in your life could safely hear you tell the truth without turning you into a spectacle? What has kept you from choosing them sooner? What are you afraid might change if you are seen clearly?

Forgiveness is also a practice of time. Expecting a full pivot in a single session is a recipe for failure.

Self-forgiveness often arrives in increments: one night where the mouth does not rehearse self-abuse; one morning where you choose a gentle action rather than a punitive one; one apology offered that lands lightly in someone's heart. Count those small loosening moments as wins.

What small sign today would tell you you are moving? Are you willing to count quiet shifts as progress? What if movement did not have to be dramatic to be real?

Ritual can be powerful. People have found symbolic acts transformational: writing a letter to your past self and burning it, taking a walk to a place that witnessed harm and laying down stones with the names of regrets, making a list of behaviours you will avoid and behaviours you will cultivate and placing it somewhere visible. Rituals make internal processes visible and thus manageable.

What small ritual might feel authentic for you … not performative, but true? What would feel honest rather than impressive? What ritual would you keep even if no one ever knew about it?

Self-compassion meditations and compassionate imagery are tools, too. Picture the younger you who made a mistake and imagine that version sitting across from you, frightened and earnest. What would you say to that child or younger adult if they were someone you loved? Many people find they can extend to another version of themselves the tenderness they cannot yet give in the present tense. Could you practice that address… gentle, steady, corrective but kind … even for five minutes a day?

Another unseen challenge is the risk of moral license. Forgiving yourself can feel dangerous if it precedes accountability. The balance is to accept discomfort as part of making amends; forgiving is not the end of moral work.

A person who hurt another may forgive themselves only after concrete change: therapy, restitution, changed behaviour. Self-forgiveness that evaporates responsibility is hollow; self-forgiveness that follows hard work is reparative.

How do you know which you are practising? What evidence do you have in your behaviour, not your intentions? What discomfort are you still willing to tolerate?

Culture complicates the matter further. Some traditions valorise endurance and penance; others promote immediate mercy. In some communities, forgiveness is public and communal; in others, it is private and internal.

Your context shapes what forgiveness looks like and what it asks of you. Which cultural scripts are you carrying that make self-forgiveness hard? Which could you question? Who authored those scripts? And what permission would it take to edit them?

We must also attend to systemic dimensions. People who have been harmed through structural privilege…say, someone who benefited from unjust systems…face a different choreography of self-forgiveness. Their path includes acknowledging complicity, dedicated acts to redistribute power, and ongoing allyship.

Self-forgiveness in those contexts cannot be purely emotional; it must be political and material. Are you prepared to turn private regret into public accountability? What would that cost you? And what would it cost you not to?

Forgiveness is not the same as forgetting. Memory can be a teacher. The aim is not erasure but integration, holding the harm in memory while not letting it calcify identity.

How would your life change if you carried memories as lessons rather than shackles? Which concrete learning can you extract from your harm that ensures it will not be repeated? What pattern are you responsible for interrupting? What vigilance will compassion require?

Finally, tenderness with yourself matters. There will be backslides. You will apologetically return to old scripts. The work is not linear. Progress and relapse braid together. Expect patience.

Practice small mercies: a forgiving sentence at the end of the day, a deliberate act of rest, a refusal to ransack your chest for evidence of worthlessness.

How might you talk to yourself tonight differently than you did this morning? What tone would feel reparative rather than corrective? Who taught you the voice you currently use?

Some practical steps you can begin today:

- Name the act. Write it down in a sentence that separates action from identity.
- Ask, "What can I repair?" and choose one small tangible step.
- Find one witness and speak the truth aloud.
- Design a short ritual to signal a release (a walk, a letter, a small offering).
- Practice a five-minute self-compassion meditation daily.
- Make one plan that turns regret into action, like volunteering, making amends, or learning a new way of being.

Ask yourself:

What forgiveness do you owe yourself that you have postponed on the altar of perfection?

What would it mean to stop rehearsing condemnation and begin rehearsing kindness?

Which part of your story can you bring into daylight and ask, not for exoneration, but for a chance to change?

What would change feel like in your body?

What would you have to stop rehearsing to allow it?

The quiet work of self-forgiveness asks for courage that is not always glorious. It asks you to witness your own failings with a steady gaze, to commit to repair where possible, to recompose your identity after harm, and to keep showing up even when the heart is tired.

Forgiving yourself does not make the past disappear. It makes room to breathe. It does not erase consequences, but it softens the interior climate enough to do the work consequences demand. It is a slow reclothing of the self…less theatrical absolution, more tailored mending.

What would it mean to let mercy be a practice rather than a verdict? And what kind of life becomes possible when self-forgiveness is no longer postponed?

In the asking, I changed.

And I learned not to disappear from my own life.

What We Never Said

We carry them quietly. Conversations that never happened, questions that were never asked, answers we never gave.

They sit at the bottom of our memory like loose change in an old coat pocket, forgotten until we reach for something else.

The words we never said echo louder than the ones we did. They shape our regrets, our anxieties, our daydreams of what might have been if we had just spoken up.

There is a physicality to this silence. It lodges in the throat, becomes a small tautness behind the ribs, a cadence of avoided syllables that replays when we are alone.

Neuroscience shows that unexpressed emotions do not evaporate … they are metabolised into patterns of avoidance and rumination. That bodily charge is why unsaid things feel heavier than ordinary memory. They are not just recollections, they are unresolved work the nervous system keeps trying to finish.

What does your body carry when you don't say the thing you've rehearsed in your head?

Why is it that silence leaves a louder imprint than speech? Why do certain unsaid things take up permanent space in our minds, sharper than insults, deeper than praise? What are we afraid will happen if we say the thing we most want to say? And what happens when we never do?

Fear and risk live in the room with us. Sometimes we imagine catastrophe ... the conversation that collapses a relationship, the confession that is rejected, the truth that stains someone else's portrait of us.

Anticipated regret often outweighs present possibility: We imagine the worst response more vividly than the best. Are we protecting ourselves from imagined harm, or are we robbing ourselves of possible repair?

My friend hadn't seen her brother in nearly a year. They'd grown up in the same cramped house with peeling blue paint on the walls and the sound of ceiling fans humming through every summer. Their bond used to be effortless, filled with shared chips during cartoons and confessions whispered under bedsheets. But adulthood came with distance, and when their father passed away, it brought silence instead of comfort.

Loss magnifies absence in strange ways. When a parent dies, the family's script stutters; people who once knew how to respond suddenly don't. The rituals of grief assume speech…eulogies, stories passed at the funeral…but sometimes grief draws people inward instead.

The silence between siblings then, is not neutrality; it is an active recalibration of roles. What does it mean to grieve together in different languages of silence?

She had wanted to ask him that day why he didn't cry. Whether he felt anything when the ashes scattered into the river. Whether he hated her for not being there in time. But instead, they sat in the car after the ceremony, windows fogged from their breath and winter rain. She looked over at him, hands on the steering wheel, jaw tight, eyes fixed ahead. Her throat tightened. She almost said something. Almost. And then the radio played a soft, forgettable song, and they drove away.

Regret is often built from "almost." Those near-sentences are what psychologists call counterfactuals … the alternate scenarios we rehearse in the imagination. Counterfactual thinking can be useful if it prompts repair; it becomes corrosive when it loops without action.

If you could go back, what is the single question you would ask? If you can't return, what tiny ritual might permit you to address it now?

What would have changed if she had spoken? Would they have understood each other better, or broken even more? Why is it easier to drive in silence than risk making eye contact with someone else's grief?

There is humility in silence sometimes … the recognition that words could harm more than help. But there is also avoidance.

The main question is:

Does your silence keep someone safe, or does it keep you comfortable?

Which stories do you owe to those you love, and which are you allowed to hold private?

There was a colleague once. A woman who always brought her office best friend the first cup of tea in the morning, slightly too sweet, always warm. They worked together for five years, shared lunch breaks and inside jokes, and protected each other from workplace drama. On her last day, when she handed in her resignation, the colleague hugged her and said, *"You were the only reason I didn't leave sooner."* But she didn't say anything back. Didn't tell her how much that daily cup of chai had meant.

Didn't tell her how the woman's presence had made office politics bearable.

So much of human connection runs on small transactions of gratitude. Gratitude is a fragile currency: it requires naming.

Social research shows that expressing appreciation not only deepens relationships but boosts the well-being of both parties. Why do we put off thanking people until after they are gone? What rituals could we practice to name the ordinary gifts while they are still being given?

Why did she hold back? What made her think she'd have more time, more days, more cups of tea?

Procrastination around speaking is not laziness … often it is the fear that the moment will be less charged if we ritualise it. We imagine that naming gratitude will demystify it, make it ordinary. Yet ordinary naming is precisely what makes bonds durable. Which small truth could you say today to someone you will see tomorrow?

I remember briefly my friend telling me about her mother. With her mother, the words were even heavier. She had grown up resenting her for being too strict, too quick to judge, too hard to please. And yet, when her mother grew older, and her hands began to tremble while chopping vegetables, all that resentment softened into a quiet guilt. She watched her mother fumble with the remote one day, the room smelled like medicines and lavender, her chest felt heavy, and all she wanted was to ask, *"Do you remember being harsh with me when I was little?"* Not with anger, just curiosity. Maybe even forgiveness.

Parents are living archives of our childhoods … both the wounds and the tenderness. The impulse to ask for acknowledgement, or to offer forgiveness, is tied to narrative closure.

Family systems therapists talk about "repair sequences": short conversations that can interrupt decades of accumulation.

What if a single curious question could shift the gravity of a relationship? What keeps us from asking it?

But she never asked. The moment passed, as it always did. The television show started. Her mother smiled faintly at the screen. All she could hear was the buzzing sound from the fridge and then … the silence grew roots.

Roots, once sunk, are harder to unearth. The longer a silence sits, the more it stabilises into identity: *"I'm the daughter who didn't ask"* becomes a script she plays out. That script then governs future opportunities for retrieval. How do you loosen roots without uprooting the person you are?

Are we protecting others by staying quiet, or are we protecting ourselves from hearing answers we don't want to know?

This is the painful fork: speaking risks a painful truth; silence risks lifelong curiosity. Which is kinder to the other? Which is more honest to yourself?

With lovers, the silence is trickier. There was one in particular. A man she had loved fiercely, foolishly, in the way only someone full of hope can love. Their conversations were always almost enough. But he never asked her to stay, and she never asked him why he didn't.

Romantic silence often carries themes of shame, fear of appearing needy, or calculations about power.

Attachment theory tells us that some people minimise needs to protect against rejection. But minimisation severs the very intimacy it aims to preserve. How might relationships change if vulnerability were practised as a skill rather than avoided as a risk?

They had one last dinner together. Candlelight cast golden shadows across the table, her red dress sticking slightly to the back of her thighs in the summer heat. He talked about a job opportunity abroad. She nodded, smiled, and kept sipping her wine. The lump in her throat stayed until dessert. She wanted to ask, *"Why don't you want me to come with you?"* but instead, she said, *"The tart is good."* He agreed. The moment was lost.

The small substitution … food words instead of the hear… is a familiar defence. Humour and triviality often displace the uncomfortable because they preserve control. What do you protect when you avoid the question? How does that protection cost you later?

Do we fear sounding needy more than we fear being unloved? What are we protecting when we choose politeness over vulnerability?

Needs are human, not defects. Reframing need as information rather than indictment might allow for more honest questions. When someone asks for presence, is the request a test or an invitation? How might you reframe your internal narrative about needing someone?

There's a queer friend I know. Confident, loud, quick-witted, always the first to break the tension in a room. One day, he quietly came out to me while we waited in line at a crowded metro station. Fluorescent lights flickered above us, and a child cried two people ahead. I said, *"Thanks for telling me,"* and hugged him. I thought I was being supportive.

Being supportive is often presumed to be a single moment of affirmation. True support is an ongoing stance: asking follow-ups, checking in later, and offering concrete help if needed.

What follow-up might a friend have offered that would have mattered? How do we learn to be reliably supportive rather than performatively so?

But later, I realised I hadn't asked anything more. Not how long he had been holding it in. Not how his family reacted. Not if he was okay. I had been so afraid of saying the wrong thing, I said almost nothing at all.

Silence born of fear often masquerades as respect. But respect without curiosity can feel like dismissal. How do we balance not imposing with not abandoning? What questions convey care without interrogation?

Can silence sometimes feel like indifference, even when it's meant to be respectful? Why do we assume kindness means keeping quiet, when sometimes it's listening that matters most?

Psychologists call it the Zeigarnik Effect. The tendency to remember unfinished tasks more than completed ones.

The same principle applies to conversations. The things we didn't say keep coming back, uninvited.

Philosophers have long debated the ethics of silence. Is withholding the truth a form of dishonesty? Can restraint be more harmful than expression?

The literature on moral silence distinguishes between permissible discretion and cowardly omission. Context matters. But the internal calculus often gets fogged by fear and habit.

How do we develop practical rules for when to speak and when to hold? Who mentors us in the ethics of saying things that matter?

I once saw a man at a hospital café, sitting across from an elderly woman with oxygen tubes in her nose. He looked young, perhaps her grandson. He held a coffee cup between his palms but didn't take a sip. She reached across the table and held his wrist.

"Have I been a good mother?" she asked.

He said nothing. Just lowered his head.

And that silence told her everything.

Some silences are answers. The non-answer can communicate complexity, shame, relief, or inability. Silence is not neutral language; it is expressive. How careful are we in interpreting it? How often do we assume silence equals malice when it may be speechless sorrow?

Do we stay quiet because we don't have the answers? Or because we know the truth but don't want to hurt them by saying it out loud?

Both motives are human. Both carry weight. The ethics of response asks us to weigh harm: sometimes the blunt truth heals, sometimes it scars. Who are we to decide which?

Unspoken words aren't empty. They are heavy. They shape how we remember people, how we interpret memories. We imagine the replies we might have received. We write both parts of the script and reread them obsessively.

There are practical exercises that help. Writing unsent letters, for example, allows you to articulate what you need to say without forcing another person into a reaction.

Role-playing the conversation with a trusted friend or therapist can help you calibrate tone and content.

Saying the words aloud in a private place can defuse the physical pressure of unsaid sentences.

Which of these tools might let you move from paralysis to possibility?

Could a simple *"I miss you"* have changed something? Would one vulnerable confession have softened a decade of distance? Or are some silences better left untouched?

We cannot know outcomes with certainty. Choice requires risk.

But we can orient toward questions that favour repair:

What is the smallest honest thing I can say that keeps the door open?

Which truth will let me sleep better tonight?

We tell ourselves we'll say something next time. But what if there is no next time? What if the moment to speak is always now?

This urgency is not meant to generate panic; it is an invitation to presence. Life's clock is unreliable. Our moral responsibility sometimes sits in the present tense. What small phrase can you risk saying today that your future self will thank you for?

I often think of all the conversations I'll never have. Letters never sent, messages typed and deleted, phone numbers still saved but never dialled. What would it cost to finally speak? And what might it set free?

Speech can set free or complicate. Either way, it is an act of agency. Even if the reply is not what we hope, the act of speaking can recompose the self from "someone who waited" to "someone who decided." Which identity would you prefer?

In the asking, I changed.

But I never learned how to carry the weight of words I never said.

Did I Say Yes, to This?

Once upon a time, in a world where a woman's ticket to a secure future was stamped with a marriage certificate, saying "I do" was less a choice and more a survival strategy.

Marriage used to be a necessity. Now, it's a choice…a choice that feels like walking into a carnival funhouse where the mirrors distort everything. One moment, it's a picture-perfect dream; the next, it's a haunted maze of outdated expectations and unspoken sacrifices.

For centuries, marriage was the only socially sanctioned means through which women could gain protection, stability, and recognition. A daughter was first shielded by her father and later by her husband. In a time when women had little access to education, property, or public life, marriage wasn't just a cultural milestone … it was a lifeline. What passed for love was often merely survival in a system that offered few alternatives.

Think of the long genealogy of customs: dowries, guardianship, the legal erasure of a woman's name in property records. Those practices taught entire generations that to be chosen was to be safe … and safety felt like success. Safety could be felt in the clink of coins at a wedding, in the formal seal of a contract, in the way relatives breathed easier. It was not necessarily tenderness; it was the solidity of having another person declared as your social anchor. That anchor carried benefits, but also gravity.

But today, the world has shifted. Women are educated, employed, and empowered. They've built their own careers, pursued their own dreams, and carved out spaces of joy and independence. And yet, despite this progress, many approach marriage with caution. Not because they fear love or commitment, but because they fear what marriage might ask them to surrender.

There is a tension between the rhetoric of modern equality and the inertia of cultural expectation. Laws change faster than habits. A woman may hold corporate titles and board seats, but still inherit the domestic default: the first to wake with the child, the last to rest after the dishes, the one whose accomplishments are footnotes at family gatherings.

The question then becomes practical: how do we align the promises of modern life with the persistent realities of private labour? How do we make institutions that used to require surrender now support partnership?

Let's look at two scenarios:

One: Arranged Marriage

She was a singer. Not just any singer … her voice stirred rooms into silence. Her concerts were sold out, her Instagram reels soared past a million views, and she glowed under stage lights, her microphone an extension of her soul. Singing wasn't just something she did; it was who she was. Then came her arranged marriage.

The image is electric: stage smoke, hands raised, the bass vibrating under skin, a moment when the room breathes with her. That bodily memory … the way applause lands like weather on the skin … becomes a measuring stick. When a marriage asks you to erase that measure, it is not only asking for time or privacy; it is asking you to disown a visible, felt piece of yourself.

At first, her husband seemed supportive, proud even. But the applause hadn't yet faded from her last show when the cracks began to show. His parents, traditional and rigid, saw her art as shameful, unsuitable for a woman now *"respectably married."* Her videos were called vulgar. Her public presence an embarrassment.

There's a distinct cruelty in the timing. It is the way admiration can reverse into suspicion, as if the same loudness of applause that once signalled talent now signalled impropriety. The family's voice is rarely a single source; it arrives in whispered comments at meals, in the soft closing of a door, in the way the television is turned on to drown out the sound of practice. These small acts of containment accumulate until the stage becomes memory, and memory becomes ache.

"Women in this house don't sing for strangers," her father-in-law had said over dinner. Her husband, who once admired her performances, scrolled through her old videos with a new frown.

"You should delete these," he said flatly.

"But this is my career," she said softly.

"You're married now," he replied. *"This family comes first."*

The language of possession creeps into the domestic lexicon so quietly that we mistake it for ordinary speech. Possession does not always arrive as violence; often it arrives as requests dressed as concern, as *"for the family's dignity,"* as *"what others might say."* Each request lights a breadcrumb trail toward self-erasure.

She drove back to her old apartment that evening. Sat in her car, hands still trembling. Her lipstick had smudged. Her favourite gold hoops dangled like questions she no longer had answers to. She stared at the screen one last time before hitting delete. One video. Then another. And then the silence.

That gesture … the deletion … is a brutal kind of grief. It is the removal not just of content, but of evidence; evidence that you were once visible, that you once claimed public air. The car around her smelled of petrol and leftover perfume; the world outside moved as if nothing had shifted. But inside the car, something akin to a small death had been performed: a line of identity erased with a thumb.

Soon, she was cooking for a family that never said thank you. Her hands, once used to gripping microphones, were raw from scrubbing utensils. Her voice, once celebrated, now hummed lullabies to herself in the kitchen when no one was listening.

The sensory world of this new life is vivid … the metallic scrape of a spatula, the steam fogging the window, the sting of detergent on cracked knuckles. Those details anchor her to the daily. They are not inherently less noble than performance; they are simply different economies of attention.

The tragedy here is not the work itself, but the absence of reciprocal witnessing. Work that goes unseen corrodes the soul in a different way than work that is deliberately chosen to be private.

The intimacy she had imagined was replaced by cold schedules. Sex wasn't romantic … it was timed around ovulation, a task with a deadline. When she once tried to reach for him, wanting closeness, he flinched.

"You smell like dishwash," he said. *"It's not attractive."* She wasn't his wife. She was the help. She wasn't his partner. She was his family's unpaid servant.

There is a particular violence to this line: it reduces the body to a commodity, intimacy to inspection. It is not merely a comment about scent; it is a boundary-setting by erasure. The language creates a hierarchy in the household that organises who is visible and who becomes infrastructure.

What had she signed up for? Was it her fault for dreaming too much? Was it his fault for shrinking her? Or was this simply what marriage had always been … a system that expected women to sacrifice without question, to disappear without protest?

There is a social grammar here that normalises withdrawal of agency: small apologies, the polite acceptance of directives, an internalised expectation that women will always compensate. These scripts can be relearned, unlearned, and rewritten … but doing so requires both awareness and practical levers: property rights, economic independence, supportive relatives, and cultural narratives that model mutuality.

And then there was another story. A different kind of beginning.

Two: Love Marriage

She had a love marriage … the kind that made friends jealous and relatives nod approvingly over cups of chai. He used to pick her up from work just to spend a few extra minutes together. They took long drives through city lights, the windows down, music from her playlist humming low. She always wore perfume … a sharp floral note that lingered in his car even after she stepped out. He loved how she dressed: soft silks that caught the light, heels that clicked confidently down marble hallways, lipstick that never smudged, no matter how long the day was.

This arc shows how love and initial attention can be intoxicating … the way small rituals (picking up from work, shared playlists) function as a tender economy. Those rituals deposit goodwill into the relationship's account. But goodwill needs maintenance; unnoticed, it gets spent and not replenished.

He told her she was luminous.

They would lie on the balcony floor some nights, sipping on cheap wine, staring at constellations neither could name. He'd stroke her hair and say, *"Promise me you'll never change."* And then they got married.

Promises like "never change" are performative in two senses: they flatter by wishing to freeze the beloved at their best, and they infantilise by asking the beloved to remain permanently static. Humans grow. Those promises can become traps, expectations that punish evolution.

Now she woke before sunrise. She tied her hair in a loose bun, not because it looked neat, but because it kept falling into the pressure cooker. She folded his shirts crisply, swept the floor before 9 a.m., and answered work calls between stirring daal. The once-perfect wardrobe grew dusty … her heels traded for flat chappals that didn't click but flapped. Her silk sarees gave way to loose cotton kurtis stained with turmeric near the waistline.

There's dignity in domestic labour; there's also invisibility when that dignity goes unrecognised. The transition from public self to domestic caretaker can be subtle and then sudden. Time that once allowed for rehearsals, rehearsals of music and self, now collapses into rituals of care.

She didn't stop caring about how she looked. She just didn't have time to.

The bathroom mirror, once lit with her ring light and scattered with makeup brushes, now reflected a tired face wiping steam off the glass. Her favourite lipstick … a deep plum … lay forgotten at the bottom of a drawer, next to a dried-up nail polish bottle and old concert tickets from the early days.

Objects become relics: the concert ticket becomes a small, sad shrine, a tactile reminder of life before the slow fade. The gesture of forgetting is not always resignation; it can be a survival mechanism…conserve emotional resources for the tasks that demand them now.

She still tried, sometimes. On weekends, she would curl her hair, dab on the perfume he once said reminded him of rain. But now he barely noticed. He'd grunt something about the groceries and scroll through his phone during breakfast.

There is a loneliness in being invisible in the home of someone who once loved your presence. It is the specific ache of gifts that matter to you no longer being received as gifts. The practice of noticing requires two participants; without reciprocity, rituals hollow.

Until one day, he looked at her across the dining table and said, *"I don't know who you are anymore."*

She blinked. Not in anger, but in quiet bewilderment. Had she changed? Or had he stopped seeing her the moment she became responsible for his happiness?

This line cuts deep because it reframes agency as loss. It suggests she is a negative space … emptying rather than becoming.

The better question might be: Who are we in partnership if not a continuing series of becoming? Relationships that treat change as a threat rather than as a living process are fragile.

Before marriage, she had been taken care of. Her parents made sure she ate well, slept on time, and took breaks when she needed them. They celebrated her wins … tiny or big. But after marriage, she became the caretaker. No one asked if she was tired. No one noticed the quiet way her shoulders had started to hunch from doing too much for too many.

This echoes a larger cultural pattern: caretaking labour often migrates toward women after union, regardless of prior roles. It's not only unfair; it's a kind of erasure of prior competence. The psychological phenomenon "identity foreclosure" can describe how a person's previous commitments get closed off when a single role (e.g., caregiver) becomes dominant too early.

He had loved her when she was someone else's responsibility … when she arrived fully-formed, made up, joyful, uninterrupted. Now that she was his, he seemed to expect her to undo herself quietly, to become small and accommodating, and to do it all with grace.

There is an odd logic here: the beloved is loved as a curated object; once the object becomes a person in shared life, the curiosity wanes. Love reduced to possession tends to reveal itself as a demand for stasis rather than a generosity toward growth.

She stood at the window one night, looking at the city lights she once loved driving through. The silence of her home felt heavy. Somewhere in the bedroom, he snored softly, dreaming perhaps of the woman she used to be. The one who had time. The one who felt loved.

The city below keeps going: traffic lights blink, vendors call, distant horns stitch a rhythm. That movement underscores her stillness. The world outside is loud and alive … a remnant of her previous life … while the life she now inhabits feels paused.

She wasn't angry. She was just vanishing.

That vanishing is not always dramatic. It is an accretion of small invisibilities: a phone call not returned, an invitation declined with a thin excuse, a hobby gradually slipping into the "before" box. The grief is cumulative and often complicated by feelings of responsibility and cultural guilt.

The modern fear of marriage is not a fear of intimacy … it is the fear of erasure. Not of sharing a life, but of being asked to edit yourself out of your own story. Marriage is no longer a necessity … it is one option among many. But with choice comes hesitation. Not because women fear love, but because they fear what they might lose in the name of it.

That fear is reasonable. Choice allows for the experiment of partnership, but not all experiments are set up with consent, boundaries, or equality. The question becomes practical: how do we construct marriages that preserve selfhood? How do we negotiate terms that protect creative life, economic agency, and the daily psychology of recognition?

So, what are we really afraid of?

Is it the men who confuse care with control? The in-laws who inherit us like unpaid interns? The cultural stories that still crown sacrifice as our highest virtue?

Or is it marriage itself … the version we've inherited … that is built on the idea that to be chosen means to give more than we get?

If marriage is to survive the modern world, it must evolve. It must become more than duty and endurance. It must become a space of renewal … not erasure. A place where women don't disappear into roles, but are seen, held, and allowed to expand.

And so, the real question remains.

Can marriage make room for the woman she is, not just the one she's expected to become?

It can, but it requires courage on both sides. It requires social narratives that valorise mutual flourishing rather than unilateral sacrifice. It requires institutions … workplaces with parental leave, legal frameworks that secure property and guardianship rights for partners … that remove the structural pressure to erase. It also requires everyday practices of language: saying thank you, noticing, asking before changing expectations, and refusing to treat love as entitlement.

In the asking, I changed.

And I realised I am not afraid of love … I am afraid of becoming invisible in it.

The Hollow "I'm Sorry"

There's a moment … the breath between confession and response … where everything trembles. You say something vulnerable, something real, and wait. What comes next often isn't silence or understanding. It's a reflex.

"I'm sorry."

A phrase so rehearsed, so universally expected, that it lands not as comfort, but as punctuation. Final. Unquestioned.

"My father passed away."

"I'm sorry."

"We broke up."

"I'm sorry."

"My parents are divorced."

"I'm sorry."

"I lost my job."

"I'm sorry."

"I found out I can't have children."

"I'm sorry."

But what does *"I'm sorry"* even mean in these moments? Is it sympathy, empathy, or simply an attempt to fill the awkwardness that stretches between grief and understanding? Is it for the speaker, or the listener? And more urgently … does it ever truly help?

I was used to it by now. Every time someone learned that my parents were divorced, their voices softened, their expressions shifted into pity like clockwork. Heads tilted, lips pressed together, and there it was … "I'm sorry."

I never knew how to respond. *"It's okay"? "Don't be"? "I'm not"?*

Because I wasn't. Not sorry. Not broken. My parents were happier apart. The household had once been filled with silence, tension so thick it pressed against my childhood self's ribs. Now, I saw my mom smile more. There was laughter in maybe two places instead of cold in one. Wasn't that a kind of freedom?

And yet, their apologies made me feel like I should be grieving. Their reaction suggested that something tragic had occurred. Did they think love only counted when it remained intact? Were relationships only successful if they endured?

Why did their sorrow weigh more heavily than my relief?

Sympathy has a strange way of handling your emotions that don't belong to you. When people said, "I'm sorry," it didn't offer comfort … it handed me a script. One where I was expected to be quietly heartbroken, even if I had already found peace.

Was I supposed to mourn something that had never really worked? Was their sadness more socially acceptable than my acceptance?

I wasn't alone in this.

A friend once confided in me: *"I dropped out of college. It just wasn't for me."* And before the sentence had even settled, someone across the room offered the classic response … "I'm sorry."

But why? My friend had never looked freer. The textbooks were gone, the anxiety lifted. She had traded sleepless nights and stomach knots for art classes and morning sunlight. Shouldn't that have been a moment for congratulations, not condolences?

An example, a woman miscarried. The loss was real, quiet, and shattering. But the people around her didn't offer stillness. They offered pity. Platitudes. "I'm sorry." "It wasn't meant to be." "You'll try again."

But what she needed was different. She didn't want noise. She wanted presence. Someone to sit beside her in the hush of it all and say: *"Tell me how you're feeling. I'm here."*

And yet nobody did that.

I remember a story about a man at a funeral … his wife's. People lined up with their condolences. "I'm sorry for your loss." Again and again. Nods. Muted thanks. A line of people saying the same five words. And then an old friend arrived, placed a hand on the grieving man's shoulder, and simply said, *"She was incredible. Tell me something about her I don't know."*

And for the first time that day, he smiled.

Sometimes the kindest thing we can offer isn't an apology. It's an invitation … to speak, to remember, to not feel alone.

So why, then, are we so quick to apologise for what we cannot control? Why does "I'm sorry" become the first tool we reach for, even when it doesn't fit?

Psychologists call it the spotlight effect … our tendency to overestimate how much others notice and think about us. When someone shares something painful, we assume it's our role to say something, anything, to patch the silence. But often, the patch makes the wound more visible. Our discomfort becomes theirs.

I began to notice it more often. When I told someone about my parents, they reacted as though I had admitted to a trauma. Their pity felt louder than my peace. And suddenly, I wasn't just dealing with her own reality … I was carrying their misplaced sadness, too.

There's also the Dunning–Kruger effect at play … a cognitive bias where people with limited knowledge overestimate their understanding. We hear "divorce" and imagine broken homes. We hear "job loss" and assume despair. We fill in the blanks with our own fear, not their truth.

What happens when the reaction we offer causes more harm than the experience itself? When our "I'm sorry" becomes a weight, not a balm?

Words aren't always kind. Sometimes, they're clutter. Unexamined phrases passed down through generations. Scripts that soothe us more than they help the one we're speaking to.

Is language sometimes a rescue attempt for our own discomfort rather than a gift to the other?

There was another moment that stayed with me. A colleague, quietly sipping tea, shared that she had recently learned she couldn't have children. The room fell silent. And then, one by one, people began to speak. *"I'm so sorry." "Maybe it's for the best." "There are other ways to be a mother."*

But all she had wanted, she later confessed, was to cry without being fixed.

To sit, unspoken, and not feel like a project in need of comforting solutions.

Are we trained to fill silences because we're afraid of them? Do we rush to speak because listening feels too raw, too uncertain? Is "I'm sorry" a reflex that protects us from the vulnerability of not knowing what to say?

And what if we tried something else?

What if we asked: *How are you feeling about that?*

What if we said: *That must have been a lot. Do you want to talk about it?*

What if we didn't assume sorrow where there was none, and didn't try to erase it where it did exist?

What if we learned to sit quietly beside someone instead of filling the space with pity?

Because the truth is, not every hard thing is a tragedy. And not every pain wants a plaster.

Some grief asks for presence, not platitude.

Some stories need space, not sympathy.

And sometimes, the most meaningful thing we can say is nothing at all … just the gentle weight of being there, without needing to fix, label, or understand.

Across cultures, rituals teach different responses to suffering … some encourage words, others silence; some demand communal lament, others private stoicism.

Anthropologists note that how a society trains its members to respond matters; ritualised listening can be as potent as ritualised speaking.

What do our cultural scripts teach us about presence? Are we perpetuating a habit of hurried consolation because it is easier than learning to listen?

Historically, expressions of condolence have varied. In many traditions, people bring food, sit with the bereaved, or perform specific rites that recognise both the loss and the community's shared responsibility. Those practices create space for grief to be witnessed without being overwritten. What lessons can modern life…with its quick texts and infinite scroll…borrow from slower, communal forms of mourning?

There is also a moral psychology here. Empathy is not automatic; it is cultivated. Active listening … reflecting back what you hear, asking gentle open questions, resisting the urge to redirect the conversation to your own analogous story … is a skill. It can be taught, practised, and normalised. Imagine a social etiquette where the standard reply to hard news was a calibrated question rather than a blanket apology. How might that change the way we carry each other?

Language matters because it shapes interior weather. A reflexive "I'm sorry" can flatten nuance into a single trajectory: from problem to condolence.

A question can widen the field, turning a monologue of suffering into a shared encounter. What small changes in phrasing might we commit to? Could we replace one "I'm sorry" a day with one question meant to hold rather than patch?

There are practical, low-barrier tools anyone can practice. A pause before speaking; a short phrase like, *"Tell me how you're feeling"*; naming what you notice… *"You look stunned"* … rather than translating the emotion into pity; offering specific help … *"Can I bring you lunch on Tuesday?"* … rather than abstract condolences. These acts shift attention from the speaker's discomfort to the other person's need. Which of these feels approachable to you? Which would be hardest?

And what about silence? Silence is not always emptiness. Sometimes it's a kind of attentive presence that says, I will sit with you even at risk of my own unease. How comfortable are we with not knowing? How willing are we to let someone's sorrow remain complex and unresolved in our presence?

There are also questions of power and gender in consolation. Studies and social observation show that some people … often women … are expected to perform emotional labour, both in giving and receiving empathy. Others are offered quicker consolations, the "there - there" responses that never land because they bypass the person's actual need. How do social roles shape the type of responses people receive? Who gets presence, and who gets platitudes?

I noticed more, too, how the pattern repeated in small moments:

A friend's job loss was met with well-intentioned but hollow phrases

A neighbour's illness summarised with an "I'm sorry" and a quick exit.

These responses do not cost much … they're socially cheap … but their cheapness is its own cruelty. The effort of true presence, by contrast, costs time and attention.

Is that why we avoid it? Because true presence requires a slowing that many of us are not taught to do?

There was a moment I treasure, quietly luminous.

A colleague shared that he'd been bullied at a previous job and was still raw about it. The team clustered for a moment, and one person said, without urgency, *"That sounds like it hurt a lot. Do you want to tell us more?"* The colleague's shoulders dropped. He talked. People listened. No grand consolations were offered; there were follow-ups, small offers of resources, and an after-lunch check-in.

The harm did not vanish, but it was acknowledged in a way that kept him human rather than a spectacle. What did that meeting teach us about the architecture of care?

Perhaps the deepest lesson is humility; to recognise that our first instinct is not always the right language. To learn that comfort is learned behaviour, not instinct. To rehearse presence the way musicians, rehearse performance … with attention, with intention, with repetition.

What would change if we taught children not to say "I'm sorry" reflexively, but to ask: *"Do you want to talk?"*

What if workplaces normalised a different scripting…a culture where offering time and listening trumped platitudes? What if families practised witnessing rather than fixing?

There are limits to what words can do, of course. Some anguish resists articulation. Some pain is private. But the habitual move to apologise as a default response robs us of a chance to be good witnesses. It centres our discomfort and turns grief into a conversational props-and-closure act.

So, practice the pause. Learn one question that opens instead of closes. Offer to sit. Bring soup. Ask permission to speak about the person who is gone. Hold your hand on a shoulder a little longer than seems polite. These gestures compound.

In the asking, I changed.

And I learned that sometimes, silence listens better than sorrow speaks.

Treadmills in the Mind

What if the first question you asked yourself each morning wasn't, *"What must I do?"* but simply, *"Who do I want to be today?"*

What would change if your opening thought were about belonging and presence, not about a tally of tasks?

These are not sentimental exercises; they are diagnostic. The stories we tell ourselves about worth … that motion equals meaning, that being busy signals seriousness … shape the architecture of our days.

Where did those stories come from? Whose approval are we vying for when we slide into motion before our feet touch the ground?

There are structural answers and tiny, practical ones.

Historically, the rhythms of human life followed seasons: planting, harvest, festivals, and repair.

The Industrial Revolution recast time into quanta: shifts, quotas, punch clocks. Work became measurable in ways it had not been before.

Later, the Protestant work ethic and Enlightenment narratives amplified industriousness into moral seriousness.

Now algorithms and apps have folded that ethic into our pockets: notifications, streaks, badges. The tools we built to save time have, perversely, extended their demands.

How did convenience become compulsion? When did rights won for rest become loopholes in a round-the-clock expectation?

There is also a physiology to habitual doing. Our brains reward small wins…a checked box, an answered message…with microbursts of dopamine. That tiny hit trains attention toward endless small tasks and away from deep, slow satisfactions. The Zeigarnik effect keeps unfinished tasks buzzing at the edges of consciousness; the availability heuristic makes the urgent feel more important than the significant.

Over time, these neurological biases become cultural habits. What would it take to retrain those habits in the service of deeper life … long conversations, careful work, afternoons that feel like belonging rather than deadlines?

It starts with the alarm clock. Not the gentle chime of awakening, but the harsh buzz that demands obedience. You open your eyes to a screen already lit with emails, a calendar marked in red, a to-do list so long it hums with anxiety. Before your feet touch the floor, you've already failed to meet the pace of the world. And yet, you move. You rush. You caffeinate. You pretend this pace is normal. Necessary. Desirable.

But when did exhaustion become a badge of honour?

We live in a world that claps louder for the person who stays at their desk past midnight than for the one who leaves on time to read to their child or spend time with the person they love.

We speak in numbers: steps walked, emails answered, hours clocked. Breaks are confessions. Vacations, guilty pleasures. Rest, something to be earned. Productivity is no longer a function of time…it is a measure of worth.

Who decided that our value should be tied to how much we can do, rather than how well we live?

There's a colleague … they, like many, have perfected the art of looking busy. Their eyes are constantly scanning the next task, their phone never out of reach, their smile permanently set to "no problem." They volunteer for every late-night deck, every extra round of edits. Praise follows them. So does burnout. But no one sees that part. No one applauds the moments they sit alone in a cab at 2 a.m., stomach knotted, eyes wet, wondering when their life began to feel like a treadmill they can't get off.

And perhaps they're too afraid to stop running. Because who are we, really, if we're not being productive?

In interviews, resumes, and even casual conversations, people wear their exhaustion like a crown.

"I haven't had a weekend off in months."

"I only sleep five hours a night."

"Work's been crazy, I haven't had time to breathe."

These aren't complaints … they're humble brags. They're declarations of commitment, of discipline, of grind. Somewhere along the way, effort became more important than outcome. Busy replaced fulfilled.

Why do we believe that doing more means we are more?

A young woman once told me about her first job out of college. She worked in the media … long hours, high expectations, little guidance. Her boss told her, *"If you want to make it, forget balance. You can rest when you're successful."* So, she tried. She skipped meals, stopped meeting friends, and her hobbies faded into irrelevance.

Every achievement came with a shadow of guilt: *"Could I have done more? Should I be sleeping less? Working weekends? Would people notice if I slowed down?"*

And slowly, they did. They noticed not her dedication, but her distance. She forgot birthdays. She missed dinner with her mother three weeks in a row. She became a stranger to the people who once grounded her. But professionally, she was doing "well." Promotions came. So did therapy.

Why do we conflate busyness with ambition, and silence with stability?

Even rest has been commodified. A break is only valid if it's "productive" … a workout, a self-help book, a meditation session you can talk about on LinkedIn. There's no room for silence unless it leads somewhere. When did being still become suspicious?

There's a friend who paints … not to sell, not for social media, just to feel something soften inside her. But every time she talks about it, people ask, *"Are you planning to exhibit your work?"* as if joy alone isn't justification enough. Even hobbies are no longer sacred. Everything must become a side hustle. Why must everything we love be monetised to matter?

In philosophy, there's a concept called instrumentalisation … the idea that something's worth lies only in its use.

We have applied it ruthlessly to ourselves. We speak of our bodies in terms of output, our minds in terms of capacity.

We forget that we are not machines. We break differently. We bleed invisibly. And when we crash, we call it burnout as if it's a minor glitch … not the soul's way of screaming for help.

Are we building a life or performing one?

We remember people for what they did. But we rarely talk about what it costs them. We admire entrepreneurs who *"slept under their desks"* but not the strain on their relationships. We quote artists who starved for their craft but ignore how many died in obscurity. We reward those who keep going…no matter the toll.

But is it truly admirable to keep running when your legs are giving way?

What if rest was a rebellion? What if choosing softness over speed was an act of courage? What if we allowed ourselves to live slower, deeper, truer?

There's a woman who left her corporate job to become a teacher. She says her days are shorter now, her income smaller, her LinkedIn less impressive. But she sleeps better. Her plants are thriving. Her smile is unhurried. *"I didn't quit ambition,"* she says, *"I just stopped outsourcing it."*

And maybe that's what this is really about … not productivity, but permission. Permission to define success on our own terms. To say, *"I am enough,"* even when we're not producing. To believe that our worth is not in how much we achieve, but how fully we exist.

What if the real accomplishment is not in how much we did today, but in whether we lived it?

If the original passage sits like a mirror in front of you, ask:

What is the first tiny habit you could change that would alter the reflection?

Could you refuse one meeting without apology?

Could you silence notifications for an hour each morning and measure the internal weather without interruption?

We imagine such experiments as indulgences, but they are forensic; they reveal the narratives driving our choices. Which narrative will you choose to believe … the one that says you must always be proving, or the one that invites you to be present?

There are public precedents for changing norms.

Labour movements fought for the eight-hour day and weekends; those gains reshaped what normal life looked like.

John Maynard Keynes wrote, almost a century ago, imagining a future where progress meant more leisure and less grind.

Thoreau walked into the woods to test what living slowly could teach him. Each of these acts … legal, intellectual, personal … recalibrated expectations. What collective acts do we need now to protect attention in an era of constant digital interruption? What institutions must change so that rest is not privatised into purchasable 'self-care' experiences but recognised as shared infrastructure?

And there are difficult realities to face. Not everyone can choose a slower life: single parents, hourly workers, people in precarious employment, those caring for elders…the treadmill can be structural, not merely psychological.

Gender matters: women still shoulder disproportionate unpaid labour, and that doubles the burden of busyness. How do we make the moral argument for rest without erasing the political work needed to make rest possible for everyone? When we talk about permission, we must also ask about policy: living wages, paid leave, reasonable scheduling, limits on after-hours expectations. Rest as a right, not only as an aspiration.

What would your city be like if designed for rhythms rather than nonstop commerce?

Imagine neighbourhoods with evening quiet hours, workplaces with no email policies after sundown, schools that educate children in the practice of presence.

Small rituals matter: a household that agrees on device-free dinners, a team that keeps one day meeting-free, a community that protects public spaces for slow conversation.

These practices ripple outward. What tiny ritual could you begin this week that would begin to change the social expectation in your circle?

Ask yourself harder questions, too. Ten years from now, what memory do you want stitched into your life? Will you be glad you answered one more email late into the night, or will you wish you'd listened to a friend without glancing at your phone?

Will your last stories be about inboxes cleared or about faces you were fully with? These are not theoretical; they are choices you make every day in how you spend attention. What will you choose?

There are practical tools that help. Block "deep work" and treat it like a meeting with yourself. Try one evening a week when you do not open your work email. Practice a short ritual … lighting a candle or making tea … to mark the end of your workday.

Learn to say "no" without overexplaining. Notice how your nervous system reacts and name the narratives that arise … fear, scarcity, the internalised voice of praise for busyness. Rehearse different stories: *"I rest because I respect my life"* rather than *"I rest only when I earn it."* Which narrative feels truer, and what does that truth ask of you?

We cannot pretend this work is easy. It will be awkward. Someone will call you Slack. A project may be lost, or a promotion delayed.

The cultural applause for busyness is loud and persuasive. But the costs of continuing to run are often higher, and less visible … relationships frayed, health sacrificed, creativity diminished. There is bravery in choosing the long game of rest, not the short trophy of exhaustive proof. Which risk are you willing to take: to be momentarily unpopular for the sake of a life that can sustain you for decades?

In the asking, I changed.

I stopped applauding my exhaustion … and began to wonder why stillness made me feel so guilty.

What If I Just Stopped Running?

What if I stopped running?

Not slowed down.

Not pace myself better.

Not learned how to manage the treadmill more efficiently.

What if I stepped off?

After years of movement, of mental sprinting, of thoughts chasing thoughts, what would happen if I simply stopped?

Who would I be if I weren't trying to keep up with my own mind?

After Treadmills in My Mind, this question does not arrive gently. It arrives breathless. It arrives with calves burning, lungs tight, sweat drying too fast on the skin. It arrives with that strange dizziness that comes not from speed, but from the moment speed ends.

Why does stopping feel more frightening than exhaustion?

Why does rest feel like falling rather than landing?

I notice how my body reacts to the idea before my mind does. The shoulders lift. The jaw tightens. There is an instinctive reach for something, anything, to hold on to. A phone. A thought. A plan.

Why does the body brace when nothing is being asked of it?

We are not built only for movement. Biology tells us this. Muscles grow in rest. The nervous system repairs itself in stillness. Memory consolidates when the mind drifts. And yet, stillness feels unnatural now. Suspicious. Almost rude.

When did stopping become a threat?

I remember sitting on the edge of my bed one afternoon, shoes still on, bag dropped where it didn't belong. The room smelled faintly of dust and fabric that had been warmed by the sun. Outside, traffic hummed, steady and indifferent. Inside, there was nothing urgent to do.

Nothing immediate.

Nothing demanding.

And yet, I couldn't sit.

Why couldn't I sit?

The mind began its quiet pacing. You should check something. You should plan something. You should use this time. Use it for what? Use it for whom?

Why does time feel owned the moment it opens up?

Rest is supposed to be restorative. But for so many of us, rest feels like exposure. When we stop moving, the noise we were outrunning catches up. The thoughts we postponed line up patiently. Fatigue stops being abstract and becomes physical. You feel it in the lower back, behind the eyes, in the heaviness of the limbs.

Is that why we keep running?

Because stopping forces us to feel what movement numbs?

Psychology calls this hyperarousal. A nervous system trained to stay alert, even in safety. The body forgets how to power down. Silence registers as danger. Stillness as loss of control.

But what are we afraid we'll lose?

I think about how often rest is framed as recovery, never as a state worth inhabiting on its own. We rest so we can return. We pause so we can resume. We lie down with one eye already open, scanning the future.

What would it mean to rest without preparing to re-enter the race?

There was a moment, years ago, when I tried to rest "properly." I lit a candle. Made tea. Sat down with the intention of calming myself. Five minutes in, I was irritated. The candle felt performative. The tea went cold. My foot kept bouncing against the floor.

Why wasn't rest working?

Because I wasn't resting.

I was monitoring myself resting.

Have we forgotten how to stop without watching ourselves do it?

We are trained early to associate worth with movement. School rewards busyness. Work celebrates overextension. Even care is framed as effort. You earn your rest. You deserve your break. You justify your pause.

What if rest didn't need justification?

When I imagine stopping completely, the fear sharpens. No goals for a while. No striving. No improvement arc.

What happens to identity when effort disappears?

This is the part no one warns you about. When the treadmill stops, the noise drops, and suddenly there is space. Space where questions echo.

Who am I without urgency?

Who am I when nothing is pending?

Who am I if I'm not trying to get somewhere else?

Stillness is not empty. It is interrogative.

I think of a woman I once watched at a railway platform. Trains arrived and left. People rushed past. She stayed seated, hands folded, eyes unfocused. Not waiting anxiously. Just waiting. Her stillness felt almost defiant.

What did she know that the rest of us didn't?

The philosopher Hannah Arendt spoke about the difference between labour, work, and action. Labour keeps us alive. Work builds the world. Action reveals who we are. But what about rest? Where does rest live in this framework? Perhaps rest is where we meet ourselves without function.

Is that why it scares us?

Stopping removes the scaffolding. Without schedules and goals, we encounter ourselves without props. No performance. No forward momentum to hide behind.

And what if we don't like what we find?

The body often tells the truth first. When you stop, aches surface. Old injuries whisper. Fatigue shows itself honestly. The body has been keeping score while the mind insisted on continuity.

Why do we call this weakness instead of information?

I remember lying on the floor once, not for exercise, not for stretching, but because standing felt unnecessary. The tiles were cool against my back. The fan above clicked rhythmically. Dust gathered in the corners of the room like it had nowhere better to be.

Lying there, I felt something unfamiliar.

Permission.

How rarely do we let gravity take us fully?

When did standing become the default?

When did lying down require explanation?

Rest is not dramatic. It doesn't announce itself. It smells like fabric softener and old books. It sounds like ceiling fans and distant traffic. It tastes like tea forgotten on the table. It is ordinary. Almost boring.

Is boredom what we're avoiding?

Boredom creates gaps. And gaps invite reflection. Reflection leads to uncomfortable realisations. Maybe we don't like the life we've been sprinting through. Maybe the speed was masking misalignment.

If we stop, we might have to admit that.

Better to keep moving.

But at what cost?

Burnout is not sudden. It accumulates quietly. The nervous system lives in a state of low-grade alarm. Cortisol hums constantly. Rest becomes shallow. Sleep no longer refreshes.

Why do we treat exhaustion like a moral failure instead of a physiological signal?

In Eastern philosophy, stillness is not laziness. It is alignment. The Tao speaks of wu wei, effortless action, which paradoxically begins with non-action. Things fall into place when force is released.

What if stopping isn't quitting, but recalibrating?

There is grief in stopping too. Grief for the version of yourself that believed speed was safety. Grief for the years spent outrunning silence. Grief for how long it took to realise rest was not the enemy.

Can we mourn that without turning it into regret?

When I stopped running, even briefly, strange things surfaced. Old memories. Half-formed thoughts. Feelings that didn't fit neatly into language. The mind, unoccupied, began to wander honestly.

Why do we distrust wandering?

The brain does some of its most integrative work in these moments. Daydreaming. Mind-wandering. The default mode network activates. Creativity and insight emerge.

And yet, we call it unproductive.

What if productivity was never the point?

Stopping does not mean abandoning responsibility. Life continues. Dishes pile up. Emails wait. But the relationship to them shifts. They stop defining the self.

Can you imagine being responsible without being consumed?

I think about the fear that stopping will make us irrelevant. That the world will move on without us. That we'll be forgotten.

But the world moves on regardless.

So why not stop?

The treadmill never cared about us. It only rewarded motion. When we step off, nothing collapses. The room remains. The air remains. We remain.

Isn't that telling?

The hardest part of stopping is not the external consequences. It is the internal reckoning. Meeting yourself without distraction. Hearing your own thoughts without editing them.

Can you sit with yourself without trying to fix anything?

This is not romantic. Some days, stopping feels like restlessness crawling under the skin. Other days, it feels like relief. Most days, it feels like learning a language you were never taught.

Rest is a skill.

Stillness is practice.

And practice is awkward before it is gentle.

When I finally stopped running, even for a moment, I noticed how loud my mind was. How much it wanted instructions. How uncomfortable it was with nothingness.

I stayed anyway.

What if staying is the work?

There is a strange tenderness that arrives when you stop pushing. A softening. A loosening. The body exhales without being told to. The mind slows its interrogation.

Moments become wider.

Time stops feeling like a threat.

Is this what we've been missing?

Stopping does not solve everything. Pain remains. Questions remain. Life is still complex. But the panic fades. The urgency loses its grip.

You begin to move again, but differently. Not propelled by fear. Not driven by comparison. Movement becomes choice, not compulsion.

What if that is the difference between running and walking?

What if stopping teaches us how to move with intention?

As the last chapter, this question doesn't demand an answer. It offers an ending that is also a beginning. Not forward. Inward.

What if I stopped running?

In the asking, I changed.

And when I stepped off the treadmill, I finally felt the ground beneath my feet.

This book ends here. The asking doesn't. "Go check *in the Asking, I Changed – 1*" if you haven't already.

And wait for 3.